THE UNIVERSITY OF SALAMANCA FROM THE MIDDLE AGES TO THE RENAISSANCE

Luis E. Rodríguez-San Pedro Bezares

THE UNIVERSITY OF SALAMANCA FROM THE MIDDLE AGES TO THE RENAISSANCE

1218-1516/29
HISTORICAL ASPECTS, POWER AND KNOWLEDGE

Translation by
J. David González-Iglesias González

EDICIONES UNIVERSIDAD DE SALAMANCA

COLECCIÓN VIII CENTENARIO, 9

© of this edition:
Ediciones Universidad de Salamanca
and Luis Enrique Rodríguez-San Pedro Bezares

© of the pictures:
Ediciones Universidad de Salamanca: figs. 1, 7, 10, 13, 15, 16, 17, 19 (author: Agustín Fernández Albalá) / 3, 9, 12, 14, 21, 25, 26, cover, flyleaves (author: José A. Sánchez Paso)
Historical General Library: figs. 12, 20, 22, 23 (author: Agustín Fernández Albalá)
University Archive: figs. 18 (author: Agustín Fernández Albalá) / 4, 5, 8
Service of Cultural Activities: fig. 24 (author: Nodal Imagen)
Office of the VIII Centenary/Ediciones Universidad de Salamanca: fig. 27 (author: Nodal Imagen)
Cathedral Archive of Salamanca: fig. 6

© of the translation:
J. David González-Iglesias González

1ª edition : October 2013

ISBN: 978-84-9012-339-3 (Print) / DL: S. 446-2013
ISBN: 978-84-9012-346-1 (PDF)
ISBN: 978-84-9012-347-8 (e-Pub)
ISBN: 978-84-9012-348-5 (Mobipocket)

Ediciones Universidad de Salamanca
http://www.eusal.es
eus@usal.es

Oficina del VIII Centenario Salamanca 2018
http://centenario.usal.es
centenario@usal.es

Cover art:
Lecturer in the sepulchre of Diego Fernández, Dean († 1303)
In the crossing of the old cathedral of Salamanca

Flyleaves art:
Detail of the coffering on the lower
floor of the Escuelas Mayores building

Proyecto financiado por el Ministerio de Educación,
Cultura y Deporte en el marco del Programa
Campus de Excelencia internacional

Layout, printing and binding:
Gráficas Lope. Salamanca
www.graficaslope.com

Hecho en España - Made in Spain

CEP. servicio de bibliotecas

RODRÍGUEZ-SAN PEDRO BEZARES, Luis Enrique

The University of Salamanca from the Middle Ages to the Renaissance : 1218-1516/29 : historical aspects, power and knowledge / Luis E. Rodríguez-San Pedro Bezares ; translation by J. David González-Iglesias González. — 1ˢᵗ ed. — Salamanca : Ediciones Universidad de Salamanca, 2013

141 p. : il. — (VIII Centenario Collection ; 9)

1. Universidad de Salamanca (España)-Historia-Hasta 1500. 2. Universidad de Salamanca (España)-Historia-Siglo 16.º. I. González-Iglesias González, David.

378.4(460.187)"…/15""15"

TABLE OF CONTENTS

THE STAMP OF AN ERA IN THE UNIVERSITY OF SALAMANCA

I F THIS BOOK, DEAR READER, is now in your hands, it is probably because you are a person interested in the history and the culture that this eight-hundred-year-old University hides between its walls. This is a history in which, as I myself have been able to confirm on several occasions, reality and legend are intertwined; hence, the importance of this work, which combines a significant effort to adapt the text to the general public with scientific rigor, and thus allows us to travel through some of the most important episodes that took place during the Middle Ages and the Renaissance, as its title reads.

I encourage you to immerse yourself in these pages and to bear in mind that they review, in a certain way, an important part of the history of this city and its main institutions along the centuries. The relation with the consecutive monarchs, the privileges that the kings granted to its classrooms since its beginnings and which became stronger with the passage of time, its relation with the Church and the intellectual atmosphere reflected in the text will help you understand the scope and importance of a University which has been and is one of the most important Spanish-speaking centers in the world since its foundation in the year 1218. It is also the oldest University in Spain to survive until our times with an uninterrupted activity since its foundation. Therefore, one way or another, the history of the University also reflects the history of the Spanish people in the last eight centuries.

This publication is another link in a collection which, thanks to the Office of the VIII Centenary of the University, is recovering and making available to the public the main documents and historical landmarks that have shaped the identity of an institution whose connections with Latin America and with the main agents of these centuries are essential to understand the evolution of our traditions. This work of recovery and exhibition is being carried out in collaboration with Ediciones Universidad de Salamanca, which contributes with its sensitivity and knowledge to provide these works with the quality standards that are characteristic of our publishing company and of the University of Salamanca.

I hope that you enjoy this book, this work that represent an important documentary reference in the illustration of a historical period that, albeit always being considered a dark one, represented a starting point of no return in which the University of Salamanca wrote some of the most important lines in Spanish and Latin American higher education.

Daniel Hernández Ruipérez
Rector Magnificus
University of Salamanca

ABOUT THE FIRST THREE CENTURIES OF THE STUDIUM

> We will have to accept that poetry can indeed correct the misprints of history and that this gullibility immunizes us against dissapointment.
>
> José Manuel Caballero Bonald,
> *Speech read in the reception of the Cervantes Prize, 2013*

RIGUROUS SCIENTIFIC STUDIES end up putting things in their place and, as a result, they also demonstrate the cunning tricks that are often introduced when establishing the historical truth of ages, people and institutions. And the history of the University of Salamanca, together with its reliable and truthful knowledge, not being beyond said trickery, requires that we actively and constantly try to establish their real terms in each period, as well as to provide a serious interpretation of their social processes all along its magnificent trajectory through no less than eight hundred years of our general history.

To this end, I introduce here the excellent study «The University of Salamanca, from the Middle Ages to the Renaissance. Historical Aspects, Power and Knowledge» carried out by Luis Enrique Rodríguez-San Pedro about the first three centuries of the Studium, which is presented in this preliminary text. The author is a professor of

Modern History of our University, an invaluable expert and a constant and fruitful researcher on its institutional influence through the Center of University History 'Alfonso IX' and the volumes of his Miscellany, both of them under his direction. Indeed, this is his first long-range work, which covers a long period that spreads from the moment of the «foundation stone», that faraway year of 1218 in which the King Alfonso IX of León «deemed it appropriate to summon wise masters on the Holy Scriptures and established that the Schools of Salamanca must be created» —as stated in the Romance language version of the Latin manuscript *Chronicon mundi*, by Lucas Tudensis, which acts as a reliable source for dating the foundation point of the University—, to the first years of the 16th century in which the «new times» of modernity are adopted, between 1516 and 1529.

The Office of the VIII Centenary Salamanca 2018 receives with great satisfaction such an important scientific initiative in the framework of its consolidated promotion and diffusion of knowledge on the history, the science, the art and the cultural heritage of our Studium. In this case, once again, we do so with the VIII Centenary Collection —which is already in the eighth volume of its series— of the publishing company of Ediciones Universidad de Salamanca, which is the clear evidence of an institutional cooperation within the University that deserves all credit.

The 13th century will witness the consecutive legal and institutional settlement of the original Scholas Salmanticae, the robust foundations of all that would be yet to come in the future. In 1243, Ferdinand III the Saint, who was already King of Castile and León, ratified the foundation of the University established by his father, and eleven years later, in 1254, his son Alfonso X the Wise wrote a Royal Order in Toledo structuring the STudium and establishing the Chairs, salaries and functions. He anticipated the creation of the oldest civil and university library in the old Europe. Finally, a bul from Pope Alexander IV granted the Studium of Salamanca in 1255 the status of Studium Generale and the *Litentia ubique docendi* for all Christendom, as he had done with the Studia of Paris, Bologna and Oxford. After the medieval period under the papal legistlative influence, the University of Salamanca entered a stage of no return in which it was subordinated to the royal power exerted by the Council of Castile through the presence of visitors and the passing of consecutive statutes.

Therefore, when our Studium faces the overwhelming frontier of eight hundred years of uninterrupted evolution, it can proudly show the privilege of being the oldest living University in Spain and the Spanish-speaking world, and also of having shaped in its own image the first American universities. Namely, the University of Lima —currently the National University of San Marcos—, which was established by the Emeperor Charles V via a Royal Order issued in Valladolid, Spain, on May 12th 1551: «[...] By this Order it is our will that a Studium Generale shall be created in the Monastery of Santo Domingo in the City of the Kings, for as long as we so decide, and that the Studium shall have all the privileges, exemptions and liberties of the Studium of the city of Salamanca».

This book is carefully structured around four great different and consecutive sections, which are naturally in accordance with the historical staging that has been established in this work and which matches the three centuries that go from the year 1218 to 1516/1529. First of all, the beginnings of the Studium Generale, the original Corporation and its development through a «precarious 14th century». Secondly, the Corporation and the Popes, the refoundation of Benedict XIII, Martin V and the Constitutions of 1422, the time of Eugene IV, the economic bases, the professors and students and the intellectual atmosphere of that period. Next come the second half of the 15th century and the Royal intervention, the Monarchs as patrons, the institutional and power aspects, and again the professors and students and the intellectual atmosphere at that time. And finally, the Kings, who assert themselves over the Pontiffs, the Royal visitors and the «new times». The text, which includes al the notes that are essential for its reading, concludes with an extensive and carefully crafted list of around two hundred references that will surely be appreciated by the readers who are eager for more information.

And to put an end to this brief introduction, I can only add a strong recommendation for those who approached the pages of this captivating book, which are to be read immediately and without delay as if it were a literary story. Aware as I am of the occasion, allow me to put it in the words of the great and much admired Caballero Bonald, who in the reception mentioned above said that «reading a book, listening to a symphony, watching a painting, are simple and fruitful vehicles that protect us from everything that prevents our access to liberty and happiness».

Salamanca, 30 July, 2013

MANUEL CARLOS PALOMEQUE
Director of the Office of the VIII Centenary Salamanca 2018
University of Salamanca

I

THE BEGINNINGS OF THE STUDIUM GENERALE

1.1. THE ORIGINAL CORPORATION

IT IS COMMONLY BELIEVED that the Schools of Salamanca were created around 1218, as has been pointed out by the chronicler Lucas de Tuy[1]. It was a Studium from the Kingdom of León, under the protection of the Monarch Alfonso IX, and it was based on the earlier Cathedral School[2]. In this regard, the Royal Chancellery maintained a close relation of mutual interest with the Cathedral chapter of Salamanca[3]. As in other cases, the Church is «the closest and most influential institution»[4] in the higher centers of knowledge, and the ecclesiastical scholars are its main actors.

This initiative was placed within a general framework of ecclesiastical education. Ever since the Third Council of Lateran of 1179, attempts were made to improve the formation of the clergy via the Cathedral Schools in which clergymen and poor students received an education. Likewise, in the Fourth Council of Lateran of 1215, Cathedrals were encouraged to appoint a master, together with a theologian, to teach Grammar and Holy Scriptures[5]. These Cathedral Schools of León from the 11th and 12th centuries show a clear French influence, because many of their teachers had been educated in France[6].

1. *Tomb of Master Randulfo († 1194), who was part of the Cathedral
School, in the cloister of the Old Cathedral of Salamanca.*

In 1135 there are already references to an «archiscola» in Salamanca. However, the data are very scarce. The question is whether the Cathedral School kept its role when the Studium Generale was created or it became part of it until it disappeared[7].

The son of Alfonso IX, Ferdinand III, King of Castile and León (which were united since 1230) confirmed in 1243 the status of the Schools created by his father (Valladolid, April 6th)[8]. He appointed the Bishop of Salamanca, the Prior of the Dominicans and the Custos of the Franciscans, among others, to settle any disputes among the students[9]. There is, therefore, a corporation of masters and students («universitas magistrorum et scholarium»). Their role is to carry out the intellectual training, and in this professional activity, the newly-formed universities are not qualitatively different from other guilds or medieval corporations linked to the cities. It is a Studium «under construction», as was the building

2. *Alfonso IX of León, founder of the Studium of Salamanca, 1218.*

3. *Tomb of the Canon Fernando Alfonso, illegitimate son of Alfonso IX of León, in the presbytery of the Old Cathedral († 1285).*

of the Cathedral in which it was located[10]. The transept and the cloister were built in the last decades of the 12th century, albeit without the chapels it currently displays. At the beginning of the 13th century, works were being carried out in some parts of the main nave, and some of the tombs of the crossing were built in the second half of the 13th century[11].

In 1254 (Toledo, May 8th), by request of the representative of the students of Salamanca, Alfonso X the Wise reorganized the Schools[12]: he appointed custodians, he provided the Chairs with funds, he regulated the rent on the houses…, and he also kept the jurisdiction of the Bishop over the clergymen of the Studium. The King recognized the ecclesiastical authority over the Schools and the bonds

4. *Letter from Ferdinand III the Saint, Valladolid, April 6th 1243, in which he confirms the privileges of the University of Salamanca.*

that link them to the Bishop and the Cathedral chapter[13]. In total, twelve Chairs were created and funded[14]: Canon law, Civil law, Medicine, Logic, Grammar and Music[15]. These Chairs were designed to fulfill the needs of the royal and ecclesiastical administration[16] in a context in which lawyers enjoyed great esteem[17].

In 1255 (Naples, April 6th), the Pope Alexander IV confirms Salamanca as a Studium Generale, by request of Alfonso X the Wise, the Bishop of Salamanca and the Cathedral chapter[18]. Also in 1255 (Anagni, July 15th), the Pope Alexander IV grants the use of their own seal to the corporation or guild of students and masters of Salamanca, by their own previous request[19]. In this same date and place, Alexander IV grants the corporation and its masters the license to teach in any analogous center in Christendom, as well as the universal validity of their titles, except in Paris and Bologna. This was known as the *licentia ubique docendi*[20]. There were other Studia Generalia in that time which were also recognized by the Pope: Paris (1246), Bologna (1253), Oxford (1254) and Montpellier (1289).

With the appearance of Salamanca, the Kingdom of León becomes part of the sphere of influence of the Italian University of Bologna, founded at the end of the 11th century (the year 1088 is taken as the conventional date) under a private and secular initiative. Bologna is mainly devoted to the promotion of the two branches of the Law («utrumque ius» or «ius commune»)[21]. In this context, it seems that the Bolognese habits and customs were adopted in Salamanca in the 13th and 14th centuries. Also, in the origins of the teaching of Law in Salamanca during the 13th century, there were important figures of masters and clergymen from Compostela who had been educated in Bologna. Towards 1275, the sons of the Bolognese glossator Accursius (Guilelmus and Cervottus) were masters in Salamanca, which serves as an example of the relation between the Studium and Bologna[22]. Finally, we may point out the establishment of a corporation of students that follow the Bolognese style («universitas

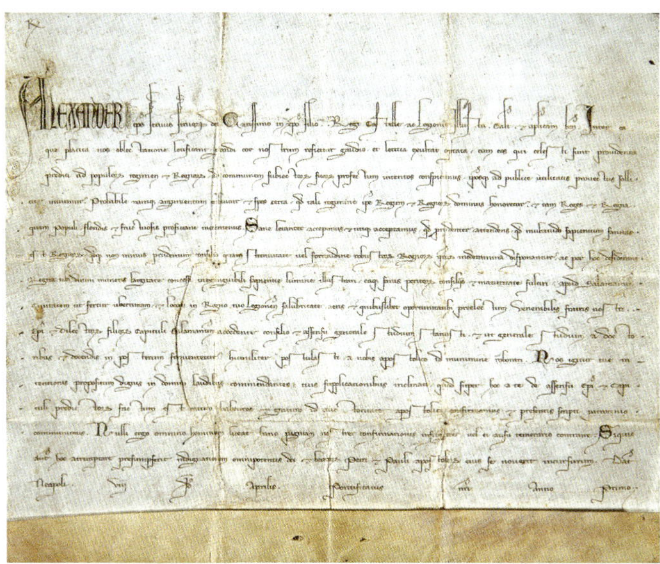

5. *Papal bull from Alexander IV, Naples, April 6th 1255, which confirms the Studium Generale of Salamanca.*

scholarium»), which will try to distance themselves from the episcopal and Cathedral connections[23].

In the second half of the 13th century, Monarchs and Popes were not overly involved. The corporation of students and masters held its meetings[24] and carried out its tasks of teaching and learning in the different fields of knowledge, with a close relation with the Cathedral[25]. There is a predominance of legal studies over other branches, and there are doubts concerning the effective implementation of other disciplines, such as Medicine[26]. There is no evidence of the existence of a University library, although both the Cathedral and some members of the Cathedral chapter had one[27]. The Kings kept on granting privileges or confirming the ones that had already been granted: there was an exemption from military service in the city and free entry of supplies and wine, the city could have its own butcher shops, etc. The ecclesiastical protection is maintained via the *Maestrescuela* (the headmaster of the Cathedral School) and the royal custodians. Among the teachers and students there is a clear predominance of lawyers and clergymen, at least those with tonsure and from the minor Orders. We do not have the articles of association or the internal regulations of the corporation, except for some vague references to their habits and customs. The royal privileges give way to a certain autonomy and independence with regard to the local civil authorities, while the papal protection makes it possible to go beyond the previous ecclesiastical limits. The funding of the institution is still based on the Tercias Reales (three ninths of the ecclesiastical tithe), and in 1286, the King Sancho IV of Castile urged the lessors to pay their dues to the University[28].

In 1298, the Pope Boniface VIII sent the *Liber Sextus* of the *Decretals* to Salamanca[29], which represents a symbolic recognition of its importance. The other Universities which received this canonic collection were Bologna, Toulouse, Padua, Orleans and the Studium of the Roman Curia. Also, Salamanca is cited in the minutes of the Council of Vienne of 1311-1312 as one of the four main Universities in Christendom: Paris in France; Oxford in England, Scotland and Ireland; Bologna in Italy; and Salamanca in Spain[30].

Next to the University itself, other centers of study were created. The Dominican friars had arrived in Salamanca around the year 1222 and there is no doubt that the monastery existed before 1229. Their relation with the University is documented since 1240[31]. Afterwards, the provincial Chapter of the Dominicans held in Barcelona in 1299 recognized the Monastery of San Esteban as a General Studium of the Order. It offered classes of Grammar, Logic and Theology. On the other hand, there are references to the presence of Franciscan friars in Salamanca in the decade of 1230, and «the barefooted» are expressly mentioned in the privilege granted by Ferdinand III to the University in 1243. At the end of the 13th century, the Franciscan monastery of Salamanca was established as a provincial Studium of the Order[32].

At the beginning of the 14th century, the Monarchs of Castile and León were the protectors and patrons of the Schools but, at the same time, their authority was interwoven with that of the Popes, who regulated the activities, recognized the graduations or made it possible to receive economic funding. Both powers granted privileges. We can establish some considerations with regard to this primitive University Corporation in the first half of the 14th century[33]. Two original nations were appointed: León, with Portugal, and Castile. An assembly of the corporation chose two Rectors, one for each nation. The assembly represents the «universitas scholarium, magistrorum et doctorum». Before the Papal Constitutions, the assembly took the decisions and the Rectors, who were appointed by the assembly, carried out its agreements. The Archbishop of Santiago supervised the income, based on the Tercias Reales of the tithe. The post of income administrator was created by Pope Clement V in 1313, and it was designated by the Archbishop of Santiago. There is a coffer for the income in the Cathedral, with several keys, in which the seal, privileges and other documents were kept. Custodians and patrons were also appointed by the Kings and referred to as «powerful people».

With regard to the economic aspect, we have certain information based on a Royal Order of Ferdinand IV from August 1300. The Monarch ordered the Tercias to be distributed to the highest bidders by the town council, the Cathedral chapter, the Bishop or one or two good men from the Church and the royal custodians. He also pointed out that the lessons were cancelled due to lack of funds and salaries. The King organized the distribution of the Tercias, which had to be guarded in a coffer in the Cathedral. The custodians were responsible for the distribution of the salaries, under the permission of the Bishop. Also, an annual accounting meeting was established, with written minutes[34].

However, there is evidence of a certain economic instability in the University at the end of the 13th century and the beginning of the 14th century[35]: the Tercias Reales from the tithe are not completely consolidated, because they had only been temporarily granted by the Popes[36]. In the first years of the 14th century, there was no money to pay the professors and, for this reason, both the town council and the Cathedral chapter had to assist the University in January 1306 with a subsidy of 12,000 maravedís. Afterwards, the Bishop of Salamanca held several negotiations until the Pope Clement V of Avignon decreed in 1313 the final allocation of the third part of the Tercias de Fábrica, which made up one third of the tithe, from the different dioceses of Salamanca to the University: the towns of Salamanca, Baños, Peña del Rey and Armuña. Their administration was supervised by the Archbishop of Santiago de Compostela[37].

There are few references to the Chairs of Salamanca in the 13th and 14th centuries, with the exception of what is mentioned in the Canons and the Laws. Several references to other matters come to an end with the administrative orders of Alfonso X the Wise in 1254, with no clear data afterwards[38]. Some authors raise questions about the teaching activity related to Medicine until, at least, the year 1313[39]. The Pope supported the missionary activities of the Dominican and Franciscan friars with Jews and Mohammedans. The 24th constitution of the Council of Vienne of 1311-1312, which was included in the *Corpus Iuris Canonici* (*Clementines* 5, 1.1), stipulated that professorships of Hebrew, Chaldean and Arabic were to be established in the Studium of the Roman Curia and in the Universities of Paris, Oxford, Bologna and Salamanca[40]. Since the middle of the 14th century we have names and fragmentary data on the lecturers of Canons in the Schools of Salamanca, some of whom came from the Portuguese territories, or from different areas of Castile, and several who were connected to the Cathedral chapter. Some of them had studied or taught in the south of France (Toulouse or Montpellier)[41].

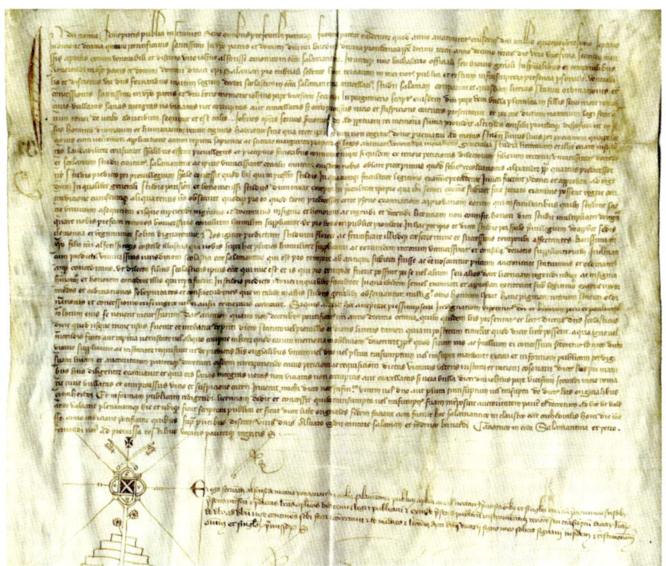

6. *Transfer of the papal bull of John XXII of 1407 in which he grants the Maestrescuela of Salamanca the power to issue Degrees. Avignon, December 2ⁿᵈ 1334.*

In 1333 (December 2nd), the Pope John XXII, by request of the King Alfonso XI and the University of Doctors and Scholars, granted the rank of Chancellor of the Studium to the Maestrescuela. The position included the power to issue Degrees on behalf of the Pope. The «licentia ubique docendi» is confirmed in all Christendom, without the exceptions of Paris and Bologna from the papal bulls of 1255. This situation progressively consolidated a sphere of authority for the Maestrescuela which «reminds of the Parisian hyerarchies»[42].

Some specialists describe a mediocre Studium of Salamanca[43] in the first half of the 14th century, with the already mentioned economic hardships, a staff made up of graduates and little influence on the Curia of Avignon, which used to appoint French lawyers for the first positions of benefices in Castile. In this regard, there were several times in which the University presented a request to the Pope in order to obtain ecclesiastical benefits and privileges for their graduates and lecturers: in the decade of 1340, for example. It was only with the arrival of Urban V of Avignon (1362-1370) that the Curia showed a certain interest in the promotion of scholars from Castile. The first specific rotulus of benefices for the scholars of Castile dates from the year 1363[44], and it was followed by others in 1365, 1366[45]... Be that as it may; the scarce number of documents in the University Archives clearly illustrates the relative precariousness of the institution at that time[46].

The evolution of the University is also related to other fields of the Cathedral. The Chapel of Santa Bárbara was founded in 1334 by the Bishop Juan Lucero; and it was afterwards linked to different University activities, such as the elections of Rectors and counselors or the degree examinations[47].

2

THE CORPORATION AND THE POPES

2.1. REFOUNDATION OF BENEDICT XIII

IN THE SECOND HALF of the 14th century, the University of Salamanca was in a difficult situation. After the great plague of 1348, a war in Castile erupted over the succession of Alfonso XI, which would put Henry II on the throne in 1369. Then, after the Western Schism (1378), Juan I of Castile chose Avignon in Salamanca and Medina del Campo (1381) with the presence of the Cardinal Pedro de Luna[48]. In that same year of 1381, once that the obedience of Castile to Clement VII of Avignon had been agreed, a general rotulus of expectative graces for the Studia of Salamanca and Valladolid was formed. A total of 342 people from Salamanca are mentioned in it, and there are references to the Chairs of Decrees, Laws, Theology (connected to the Franciscans)[49], Music and Grammar[50]. On the other hand, we also have evidence that some incumbents of the Cathedral of Salamanca were studying in Avignon in those final years of the 14th century[51].

As a pontifical legate, and later on as the Pope Benedict XIII (1394), Pedro de Luna would definitely favor the Studium of Salamanca[52]. In 1381, he already promoted a first set of Constitutions that are now lost[53], and which we can infer by their later reform of 1411. These Constitutions of 1411 were granted by the Pope Benedict XIII on the 26th of July 1411[54], after he was quashed by the Council of Pisa in 1409[55].

7. Gothic coats of arms of Castile and León and of the Pope Benedict XIII (1394-1417) on the eastern façade of the Escuelas Mayores building.

The debilitation of the monarchical powers of the Crown of Castile in the 14th century, which lacked an effective authority in some periods, was joined by the support given by the papacy of Avignon during the Western Schism (1378-1417). The papacy was interested in creating bonds with academic centers that were in favor of its cause[56]. On the other hand, a stronger connection with the pontifical power guaranteed the granting of ecclesiastical positions, benefices and plenty of privileges for lecturers and students[57]. From this point, the Studia or Universities of Castile and León strengthened their relations with the pontifical Curia and the Pope of Avignon himself became a reference for the consolidation of the University of Salamanca since the end of the 14th century. The papal influence remained after gradual measures of monarchical control were established during the reign of the Catholic Monarchs.

The Constitutions of 1411 represent the first organized and coherent legal corpus that has survived until our days. Some authors have suggested that they were created at the instance of Benedict XIII himself, who imposed his criteria without the opinion of the University corporation; hence, their reputation as a strict code. They specify the programs of their studies, with the inclusion of the Faculty of Theology; the status of the staff and the academic authorities is established; and general disciplinary regulations are set out, with a marked strengthening of the figure of the Maestrescuela. It is even probable that the final text included regulations that were already present in the previous draft of 1381[58].

These Constitutions of 1411 represent the strengthening of the two powers in the Studium: the Rector and the Maestrescuela. The previous dual rectorship (León and Castile) became unified, and the figure of the representative territorial counselors appears[59]. We may talk about four diocesan territories, two from León and two from Castile. The members were chosen via a co-optation of the outgoing members. The Rector and his counselors (*consiliarios*) assume different powers over the general assembly of the guild: they control the academic and teaching areas; they overview the absences of the teachers; they guard the chests with the treasury; they organize the meetings of the corporation (together with the Maestrescuela). The Rector and his counselors had to be unmarried clergimen, older than 25, and they could not come from or live in Salamanca. The election of Rector was proclaimed in the Chapel of Santa Bárbara of the Old Cathedral, and the process could give rise to disturbances and armed confrontations[60].

The Constitutions of 1411 establish that the Maestrescuela is responsible for maintaining order in the Studium[61], and that he has jurisdiction over it. It seems that, previously, in the Constitutions of 1381, the Archbishop of Santiago had been the person in charge of those tasks, which would later lead to demands on his part. At this moment, the authority of the Maestrescuela is reinforced, he becomes the immediate delegate of the Pope and he does not depend on any other lower ecclesiastical authority, such as the Bishop or the Archbishop. For this reason, the Maestrescuela had to be a doctor in Laws (either Canon or Civil), or a Master in Theology[62].

These Constitutions of 1411 also establish the creation of a staff of doctors and masters presided by a chairman (*primicerio*), in order to offset the preponderance of the students in the University models inspired on the example of Bologna. The text establishes a set of scholarly clothes, different from the secular garments, as well as the clothes and emblems of doctors and masters.

The Constitutions of Benedict XIII granted facilities so that Canon law graduates could graduate in Civil law by attending classes of Laws for three years. This is a sign of the importance that Roman law was progressively gaining, even for the clergymen[63].

The Maestrescuela of Salamanca, Gómez Fernández de Soria, addressed the Monarch of Castile, Juan II, and asked him to endorse and accept the papal Constitutions of 1411. The King agreed[64], but he refused to acknowledge the appointment of pontifical custodians.

For Mariano Peset, the final stages of the life of the last Antipope of the Schism were devoted to Salamanca[65]. In 1413, resources are assigned for the construction of the Escuelas Mayores building that had been designed in 1411[66]. In 1416, the funding of the Academy is reinforced, and Benedict XIII confirms the allocation of two thirds of the Tercias de Fábrica from the territories of Armuña, Baños and Peña del Rey to the University of Salamanca[67]. In that same year, he consolidated the teachings of the Faculty of Theology[68]. During these years, different academic orders and regulations were enforced[69].

With regard to the new buildings for the Schools, there are some considerations that must be taken into account. Previously, in 1378, the documents refer to the *Escuelas de Decretales*, or Schools of Decretals, «which are next to the church»[70], similarly to other existing Schools of Laws. These Schools of Laws were located, in the decades of 1370 and 1380, in the current square of Patio Chico, next to the Old Cathedral. On the other hand, we know that, towards 1417, the Schools of Grammar were located next to the Monastery of San Vicente[71]. All these premises and houses were rented by the Cathedral chapter. However, in 1411, Benedict XIII is already planning the construction of new buildings. The plans included seven classrooms or auditoriums: four of them for Laws and three for Theology, Medicine and Philosophy[72]. Afterwards, in a bull of September 13th 1413, the Pope authorized the use of a surplus fund of 2,000 florins to rent Tercias in order to start the construction of the classrooms. The work probably started in 1415, and it was finished by May 1420: «with a gallery and a courtyard in the middle»[73]. On the other hand, in 1413, the King Juan II of Castile authorized the construction of the Hospital of the Studium in the so-called House of the Midrás, or the Jewish house of prayer and study[74]. There are also references to the purchase of plots of land to build the Escuelas Mayores in December 1414 and December 1418. The first buildings of the Escuelas Mayores probably were a group of Mudejar rooms made with masonry, bricks and wooden coffering around a central courtyard. And the same design must have been used for the early Hospice and Escuelas Menores.

With regard to the economic funding, the Tercias of the first decade of the 15th century ranged between 170,000 and 180,000 new maravedís (the currency unit in Castile). This income was supplemented by the collections, a sort of contribution that was demanded from the students by the professors when their salary was insufficient to cover their needs[75]. According to the book of Tercias of 1406, the total value of the tenured Chairs was 72,170 old maravedís per year, which were equivalent to 120,283 new maravedís[76].

Apart from the figure of the Pope Benedict XIII, we have to stress in this period the presence of Diego de Anaya y Maldonado, from Salamanca, who had very good connections with the court of Castile at that time and who was Bishop of Salamanca since 1392. In the year 1401, Anaya promoted the creation of the hall of residence of San Bartolomé. He gathered a group of law

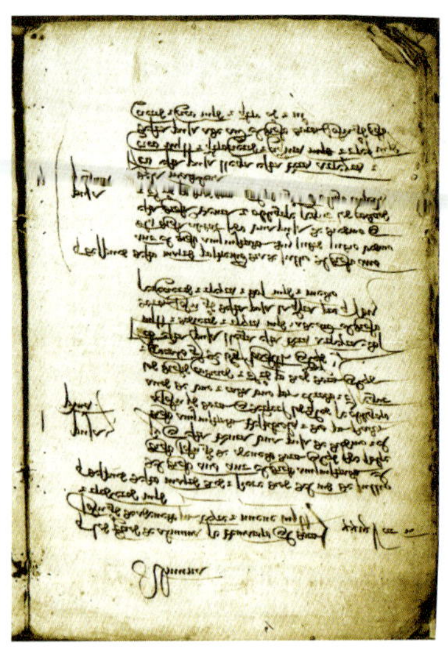

8. Book of Tercias, 1403-1408. Tercias of Armuña, 1403.

students and put them in the houses next to the episcopal palace under the authority of a Rector: the graduate Pedro Núñez. The College of San Bartolomé was created in the context of the measures taken by the Avignon papacy and of the necessary development of its ecclesiastical and administrative mechanisms. Their objective was to train a group of specialists in Law and Theology who were at the service of the interests of the Church[77]. In 1407, Benedict XIII appointed Diego de Anaya as the Bishop of Cuenca, and in November 1414, he approved the establishment of the College of San Bartolomé. In 1417, Anaya headed the delegation of Castile in the Council of Constance, and he did not hide that his initial sympathies lay with the Avignon Pope. Between 1417 and 1420, there are references of a visit of Anaya to Salamanca after his return from Constance[78], and during that visit, he inaugurated the new College of San Bartolomé, whose buildings had been under construction since 1413.

Meanwhile, there were constant clashes between different factions of the University, with the involvement of the urban authorities[79]. The town and its people tried to condition and take advantage from the University posts and decisions, and while this happened, the clashes and bribes followed one another. For this reason, in 1421, the King Juan II of Castile recognized that the University had the right to move to a different city[80], with all its privileges. These were the privileges that were sometimes challenged and sometimes hampered by the authorities of the town council and by the citizens[81].

2.2. MARTIN V AND THE CONSTITUTIONS OF 1422

With the end of the Schism of Avignon, the pontifical authority of Benedict XIII was called into question and the Roman line was reestablished with the appointment of Martin V. The new legitimized Pope would get involved by request of the University[82] and he promulgated new Constitutions in Rome on February 20th 1422, by virtue of his normative authority[83]. The committee for their creation included representatives from Salamanca, and the

9 *Coffering of the hallway of the Escuelas Mayores. Alfarje panelling with ornamental geometric interlaced pattrn (ataujerado), first third of the 15th century. Restored in 1871.*

results were supervised by the Roman Curia. However, a comparative analysis between the Constitutions of 1411 and 1422 shows some relevant similarities and continuities. The Constitutions of 1422 are articulated with the same outline as their predecessors. They recapitulate the current customs and they introduce certain changes and innovations. The text legalizes and consolidates the privileges and Constitutions created by Benedict XIII, because since 1417 in the Council of Constance, Martin V had been recognized as the only head of Christendom[84]. In the Constitutions, the Pope considers Salamanca as «one of the four Studia Generalia in the world [...] which shines in the Spanish region with a singular reputation»[85].

Now, a change in the organization of the corporation will take place. The concentration of power in the figure of the Rector, according to what was established by Benedict XIII, is no longer enough, and a Senate (*claustro de diputados*) is created (Constitution 33) in order to reach a balance between teachers and students (a restricted senate), which would replace in the majority of cases the general assembly, in which the students were a predominant force. That was the end of the open meeting of students and masters, under the argument that a few wise men elected by all would be able to obtain more results than a confused and conflicting crowd. The government of the Studium was centered in this Senate of representatives or definitors. The Senate was made up of the Rector, the Maestrescuela, ten tenured professors (chosen from among themselves) and ten students, appointed every year in the assembly meeting among a group of noblemen, dignitaries, graduates, bachelors or students without a degree. The representatives (*diputados*) met twice a month and they would reach their agreements by a two-thirds majority. If an agreement could not be reached, then the general assembly of the corporation would be consulted, which means that the powers of this last organization were greatly reduced. The tenured professors gained more influence.

Since the appearance of the papal Constitutions of 1411, the assembly of scholars did not elect the Rectors directly.

Instead, they were co-opted by the outgoing Rectors and counselors. The Rector would come from León and from Castile in alternate years. They had to be unmarried clergymen, older than 25, and they could not come from or live in Salamanca[86], according to the Constitutions of 1411. However, these new Constitutions stated that they also must not be professors. They would be chosen by co-optation in the eve of St. Martin's Day in November. Afterwards, all the members of the University swore obedience to the Rector as the head of the corporation («in licitis et honestis»)[87], and the names of the Rector and his counselors were registered in a yearbook which was kept in the chest. They had jurisdiction in all academic matters: lectures, classrooms, Chairs…

The Constitutions also detail the dioceses and the governance of the municipal territories (1st Constitution). The Kingdom of León is divided into two territories: Galicia (including Astorga and Portugal) and the rest of the Kingdom. New Castile and Andalusia made up the third territory, and Old Castile, Navarre, Aragon and the other foreign kingdoms made up the fourth[88].

10. *Stone plaque dedicated to Pedro de Luna, Pope Benedict XIII, in the low cloister of the Escuelas Mayores building.*

In the Constitutions of 1422, the Maestrescuela, which was previously elected by the Bishop and the Cathedral chapter, was now chosen by the academic Senate of the University[89]. The Maestrescuela is appointed as the guarantor of the Constitutions, statutes and norms of the University, with the power to use all the ecclesiastical censures, with full and free authority and no possibility of an appeal[90]. Therefore, the University has two heads: the Rector, representative of the corporation; and the Maestrescuela, representative of the Pope.

With Martin V, the appointment of the income administrator is no longer performed by the Archbishop of Santiago. Now, the University appoints the administrator and the Archbishop confirms the appointment. The administrator now has jurisdiction over the debtors and lessors. Consequently, the Archbishop of Santiago lost the control over the income that had been granted in the Constitutions of Benedict XIII, and he protested before the Pope.

Therefore, in Salamanca, the jurisdiction of the Maestrescuela coexisted with those of the Rector and the income administrator, who were recognized by the Constitutions of 1422: the Rector had jurisdiction over academic matters, lectures, classrooms, examinations...; the administrator had control over matters of taxes, income, lawsuits and debtors.

The Constitutions of 1422 do not detail the plan of ordinary lectures of professors and tenured professors. However, the 13th Constitution establishes that they must publicly repeat annually the lectures of the academic year.

With regard to the assignment of Chairs, the 26th Constitution of Martin V established that they were appointed by the votes of the students[91]. In the Constitutions of Benedict XIII of 1411, this was only detailed for substitute professors (11th Constitution), but it seems that this custom was also applied for ordinary Chairs, following the Bolognese tradition[92].

The regulations stated that the examinations for a degree had to be taken in the Cathedral, with an examining

11. *Original manuscript of the* Constitutions *of Martin V in the year 1422.*

board of masters and doctors who would intervene during the exposition and would vote on the suitability of the bachelor. The degrees of doctor or magister did not involve any academic requirement, and they merely were a festive (and expensive) celebration of the degree[93].

The 30th Constitution established that the income of the University had to be invested in salaries, purchase of books, maintenance of the library building, classrooms and all other construction repairs. In case there was any surplus left after these expenses had been covered, one half would be kept in the chest for any unforeseen expenses and the other half would be distributed as a «remainder» among the tenured professors[94].

The intervention of Martin V was not limited to the Constitutions. In 1421, he financially ratified the Tercias de Fábrica, which were the economic means of support of the University[95]. Sometimes he appointed professors directly[96]. He also granted many permits to graduate outside the Studium of Salamanca[97]. These permits were justified by the high cost of the degree in Salamanca, and they exempted the student from his oath to graduate in the University. This fact was seen with concern by the University, which saw its corporative privileges debilitated. Also, the Pope allowed professors to retire after ten years of teaching[98].

We can conclude that the Studium Generale of the end of the 14th century and the beginning of the 15th century received a clear protection from the Pontiffs. Many bulls were promulgated[99]. Benedict XIII created a regulatory framework with his Constitutions of 1411, which were redesigned and corrected by Martin V. These Constitutions of 1422 were registered in the Compilation of 1625 and their general guidelines were still in force until the enlightened reforms of the 18th century.

2.3. The time of Eugene IV

It is interesting to emphasize, also, the later intervention of other Pontiffs, such as Eugene IV. He is responsible for the bull of 1432[100], in which he confirmed in perpetuity the privilege of the teachers and students to receive the full benefits and dues of their posts while they remained in the Studium of Salamanca. And, likewise, he established the retirement for all tenured professors who had lectured during twenty years for eight months in each year after graduating as masters or doctors. Eugene IV himself appointed pontifical custodians of the Studium in a time when the royal protection was precarious; but they proved to be inefficient and they later disappeared[101]. The same Pontiff granted back to the University staff the prerogative to appoint the Maestrescuela in the year 1439[102].

The Archbishop of Santiago, Lope de Mendoza, complained about the Constitutions of 1422 due to the decrease in his powers, and he started a legal dispute against the University in the Curia. The Pope Eugene IV agreed to review the Constitutions[103] between 1433 and 1440, and the results favored the Archbishop. However, after the death of Lope de Mendoza in 1445, the University managed to get the same Pope to abolish those reforms and to adhere strictly to the Constitutions of 1422[104].

Nevertheless, we must take into account the fact that all along the 15th century there was not always a consensus regarding which of the pontifical Constitutions must prevail, either those of Benedict XIII from 1411 or the ones of Martin V from 1422. Those doubts were voiced in a meeting of the Senate of 1466. It might be said that, sometimes, both Constitutions coexisted[105].

With the Popes Martin V and Eugene IV, the number of people from Castile who travelled to Rome multiplied. Visits to Italy replaced the previous visits to France in the period of the Avignon papacy. Ecclesiastical benefits were sought as a reward for the academic efforts. In the majority of cases they were canonists, because Theology was not promoted among the lay clergy[106]. On the other hand, the relocation of Pope Eugene IV to Florence also had an influence on the travels to the Curia by humanists from Castile and Salamanca, attracted by the fame of the Italian masters[107].

2.4. Economic bases

The construction of the building of the University would not have been possible without the economic support of the Pontiffs. In 1381, Clement VII donated King Juan I of Castile one third of the Tercias de Fábrica from his entire kingdom for having defended his cause against the attempts of Urban VI. The King transferred that allocation from the city of Salamanca and its territories to the University, which means that the University finally got two thirds of the Tercias, because they were added to the one granted by the Pope in 1313. It was increasingly difficult to collect the payment of these two thirds of the Tercias, and the University asked Henry III of Castile in 1397 to exchange the third part of the Tercias from Salamanca for those of Armuña, Baños and Peña del Rey, which he did[108]. All these measures were confirmed by Benedict XIII (bull of Peñíscola, March 31st 1416), which meant that the University of Salamanca would from that moment on enjoy one third of the Tercias de Fábrica of the diocese (one ninth of the tithe), plus another third of the Tercias (two ninths of the tithe in total) from Armuña, Baños and Peña del Rey[109].

This marks the final consolidation of the Tercias as the main source of income for the University at the beginning of the 15th century, both for their management (renting), their volume (it was the most important resource of the University), their use (priority remuneration of tenured professors) and origin (Bishopric of Salamanca, including Medina del Campo)[110].

An entire property model was structured, and it remained in force until the end of the *Ancien Régime* in Spain. The economic management was structured around the figure of an administrator, who was in charge of general accounting, and the University coffers, in which the deposits and withdrawals were materialized[111]. The final supervision of the process was the responsibility of the Senate.

The Tercias were rented and put out to tender by the University each year, and they were assigned to the highest bidder[112]. If the bidder did not fulfill his obligations, the

12. *Seal or coat of arms of the University on the vault of the second entry hallway to the Escuelas Mayores building, 1509-1512.*

University initiated proceedings against his assets. This renting system was more convenient for the University, because it no longer had to worry about collecting, transporting or selling the income of the tithe, it saved on expenses and it received in April, June and September the earnings from the renting in cash[113].

With regard to the trends, in the first half of the 15th century, for which there are data[114], an increase in the values of the Tercias is registered, which involves a certain degree of inflation. Recessions are also present and, with them, fluctuations: 1437 and, to a lesser extent, 1441 and 1442. Between 1403 and 1408, the annual average of the income from the Tercias was of 174,775.5 maravedís; between 1435 and 1439 it was of 281,393.8 maravedís; and between 1440 and 1445 it was of 357,107.5 maravedís[115].

A «prize» for the bidders was subtracted from the total amount of the yearly income that came with the renting of the Tercias, and this created the so-called «common fund». The basic wages of the professors and other workers that had been established in the Constitutions of 1422, together with some of the expenses were subtracted from this fund. The surplus or «remainder» was distributed in two equal halves, one for the general expenses of the University and the other one for the twenty-five tenured Chairs that had been consolidated in the first quarter of the 15th century. On the other hand, the funding of the tenured Chairs was not equitable, and they perceived their proportional share according to a distribution system based on their assessment in «florins» from the pontifical Constitutions. Those florins were used as an accounting system that, once it was divided by half of the remainder, provided the real payment of the twenty-five tenured Chairs that received the yearly «remainder». This is how these Chairs always kept a large proportional share (half of it, no less) of the most important income of the University estate[116].

Even so, the horizons and economic possibilities of other destinations in the courts of Monarchs or Lords or in ecclesiastical environments or the Curia conditioned the fact that several teachers of this period and the next one abandoned or left their Chairs. For many of them, the ecclesiastical career or a promotion in the civil administration or even at the service of some powerful Lord were more attractive possibilities than the academic monotony, with its lights and shadows.

2.5. PROFESSORS AND STUDENTS

Let us now consider what the general overview of the funded university Chairs or professorships was. The books of Chairs and Tercias of 1406-1407 mention twenty-three Chairs, three of which were extraordinary because they depended on the existence of enough resources to fund them. In the Constitutions of 1411 there are still 23 Chairs, but the four extraordinary professorships turn into regular ones thanks to the consolidation of their salaries[117]. The Constitutions of Martin V do not state the number of Chairs, but ten years later, around 1432, twenty-five professorships are mentioned[118].

The number of chairs of Law in Salamanca had risen to eight, according to the rotulus by Clement VII on August 9th 1393: Prime Chair of Decrees, Vespers Chair of Decrees, Prime Chair of Decretals, new Prime Chair of Decretals, Vespers Chair of Decretals, new Vespers Chair of Decretals, Prime Chair of Laws and Vespers Chair of Laws. That is, the studies had clearly focused on Canon law[119]. Towards 1406-1407 there were nine Chairs of Laws: Decrees, two Prime Chairs of Canons, two Vespers Chairs of Canons, two Prime Chairs of Laws and two Vespers Chairs of Laws. In January 1441, one of the Vespers Chairs of Canons turned into a Clementinae and Sext Chair with the authorization of the Pope Eugene IV[120].

In Theology, there were three University Chairs, according to the Constitutions of 1411: Prime, Vespers and Bible. There were also lectures of Theology in the cathedral, but those who attended the lessons there did not aspire to a degree. Through the bull «Sincerae devotionis» on March 16th 1416, Benedict XIII reorganized the Faculty of Theology of Salamanca, as a clear alternative to the University of Paris, which opposed him. Five Chairs were established, three in the University (Prime, Vespers and Bible) and an extra two (which were added with no assigned salary) in the mendicant Studia of San

13. *Chapel of Santa Bárbara in the cloister of the Old Cathedral, 14th century. The graduate exams took place here.*

Francisco[121] and San Esteban[122]. The courses imparted in these two centers were valid in the University and vice versa. With regard to the economic aspects, since 1418, the salary of the Prime Chair of Theology was put on a level with the salaries of the Prime Chairs of Canons and Laws[123]. For their part, the Constitutions of 1422 promoted a progressive introduction of Chairs of Theology in the different monasteries and convents which would be associated to the University, like in Paris[124]. Also, afterwards, the observance of the Franciscans led to the withdrawal of the friars from the University from 1435[125]. As a result, the Chairs of Theology of the University were distributed from that moment on among the secular clergy and the Dominicans, with the exception of some non-observant Franciscan professors[126].

Since 1254 there were two Chairs of Medicine in Salamanca, a Prime Chair and a Vespers Chair. And, since that same date, two Chairs of Logic, divided into Summulae and Logic. At the end of the 14th century we can find a Chair of Physics and, in the book of Tercias of 1406 there are mentions to another Chair of Ethics, which was extraordinary and became a regular Chair in 1411[127].

The two Chairs of Grammar from 1254 are maintained, and in 1406, there are extraordinary Chairs of Music, Hebrew or Languages, Rhetoric and a third Chair of Grammar. The Constitutions of 1411 add a tenured Chair of Astrology, Geometry and Arithmetic[128].

The teaching methodology was the standard one in European medieval universities: lessons or lectures of authorized texts, repetitions or complementary conferences; and disputes or public discussions with arguments and objections, in order to develop the dialectic ability of the students. In the case of the Faculties of Law, we even have a specific method that was created by Juan Alfonso de Benavente in 1453[129].

All along the 15th century, a series of temporary Chairs appeared, assigned to graduates, which dealt with different subjects that were not included in the ordinary lectures and Chairs. They did not receive a salary from the University until 1439. Meanwhile, collections among the students were organized in order to defray the expenses of the lessons[130]. Holders of tenured Chairs were obliged to teach for eight months per year, and the remaining teaching periods were supplied with standing lecturers.

The Constitutions of Martin V opened the possibility of private lessons from bachelors. They could give classes which would count for the teaching years they needed to graduate[131], and they could do so even from their houses, although the beadle of the University had to announce the lessons beforehand.

Vacancies in the tenured Chairs (from a total of twenty-five in the first half of the 15th century) were occupied with a system of votes from the students, who chose their teachers. However, in the context of the struggles between the factions of nobles in the town, pressures, violence and impositions were commonplace, and the intervention of the King did not manage to stop them[132].

These are the requirements for graduating according to the Constitutions of 1422[133]. The students had to be well versed in Latin in order to start the courses in the faculties — «In grammaticalibus» —; because lessons were imparted in Latin, and the lectures and discussions were also held in that language. Jurists had to study for six years and teach ten lessons before they could become bachelors or

14. *Bachelor Luys Yanes († 1440), son of Pedro Yanes bachelor. Parish of St. Martin, the Epistle aisle.*

15. *Façade of the Halls of Pan y Carbón, or the «oldest Halls of Oviedo», 1386.*

bachilleres. Bachelors had to teach for five years in order to become graduates. In order to become bachelors in Medicine, students previously had to become bachelors in Arts, then study for four years and teach ten lessons. Bachelors in Medicine had to teach for another four years, with four months of medical practice in each year in order to become graduates. Students who wanted to become bachelors in Arts had to attend classes for three years and teach ten lessons. In order to become graduates, Arts bachelors had to teach for three years: one year of Logic, one year of Natural Philosophy and one year of Moral Philosophy. With regard to Theology, the University of Salamanca asked the Pope Martin V in 1419 to make the conditions and requirements for bachelors and graduates the same as in the University of Paris[134]. The Constitutions of 1422 established that bachelors in Theology had to be bachelors in Arts and study Scholasticism and Bible for five years and teach ten lessons. Then, bachelors in Theology had to teach Bible and Sentences for four years in order to graduate.

With regard to the institutions that were associated with the University, in 1386, Gutierre de Toledo, Archbishop of Oviedo, had founded the Halls of Pan y Carbón in Salamanca, the first secular hall of residence of the town[135]. And, as we have already mentioned, the College of San Bartolomé was built approximately between 1401 and 1418.

With regard to the social aspects, in these decades of the second half of the 14th century and the first half of the 15th century, there is a predominance of students from the Kingdoms of Castile and León and Portugal. Also, there are more clergymen than lay students, especially Canons. In this sense, the benefices that required a legal or theological specialization became widespread among Cathedral churches[136]. Canonists were a majority during the second half of the 14th century and the first half of the 15th century. The students came mainly from Galicia, León, Old Castile, La Rioja/Basque Country, Extremadura, Toledo and Portugal, and some groups came from Andalusia.

2.6. Intellectual atmosphere

Until the 15th century, no renowned canonists can be found in the University of Salamanca. We can only mention the figure of Petrus Ioannis, who probably worked as a lecturer at the beginning of the second half of the 14th century[137]. The teachings and writings of these jurists of the 15th century were inscribed in the sphere of Common law (*Ius Commune*), which had Roman-Canonic roots, as was the case in the rest of universities in that period. On the other hand, these Canon studies were predominant in the University. They facilitated positions and posts in the Church and the Royal administration, and at the same time they could be more easily afforded through the possession of ecclesiastical benefices[138].

The legal science revolved around the Decrees and the consecutive pontifical Decretals, as well as around the Justinian compilation, complemented with references to the codices and laws of the Kingdom of Castile: the *Fuero Juzgo*, the *Fuero Real*, the *Partidas* and the *Ordenamiento de Alcalá*. The jurisprudence was drawn from the Italian authorities in the two laws, both from the glosses and the experts on legal commentary[139]. These jurists from the first two thirds of the 15th century employed the methodology of the so-called «mos italicus», with knowledge and argumentative resources from the Bible, the Fathers of the Church, and the Classical Latin authors and historians. The reference to this last group was especially true in the case of particularly cultured authors, such as Alonso de Cartagena, Rodrigo Sánchez de Arévalo, Alfonso de Madrigal or Juan Alfonso de Benavente[140]. However, this did not mean that they could be classified as humanist authors, if we define «humanism» as a criticism to the authorities of the glosses, their methods and their writings. This school of thought would only be born at the end of the century with Elio Antonio de Nebrija.

We may add that jurists who worked as university teachers, both canonists and civilists, wrote very few texts in this period, and they also did not create prominent schools of masters and disciples. Permanence

16. *Chapel with the sepulcher of Diego de Anaya († 1437) in the cloister of the Old Cathedral.*

in the University represented an uncertain destiny, and promotions to ecclesiastic and royal positions with higher salaries and recognition were generally preferred. For that reason, many distinguished jurists lost their connection with the University[141].

Canonists from Salamanca in the first half of the 15th century were mainly conciliarist; that is, they defended the supremacy of the Council over the authority of the Pope[142]. That was the case, for example, of Juan González de Sevilla, professor in the Prime Chair of Canons and with a very close association to Diego de Anaya[143]. For that reason, the University presented a clear international projection in the 15th century in the Councils of Constance (1414-1418) and Basel (1431-1437)[144]. In Basel[145], the clash between conciliarist theorists and the papal authority became heated, and the deposition of Pope Eugene IV was even proposed in June 1439[146]. In view of this situation, the delegation of Castile, advised by Alonso García de Santa

María, withdrew from the Council[147]. The University of Salamanca had entrusted its representation to Master Juan Alfonso de Segovia, whose opinions were opposed to those of the Pope Eugene IV, although ironically, Salamanca would subsist and become consolidated as a University thanks to the determined papal protection during the first half of the 15th century[148]. With regard to the Council of Ferrara-Florence[149], the Universities of Salamanca and Valladolid did not send representatives, by command of the King of Castile, although their presence had been requested in the papal bulls of 1437[150].

Juan Alfonso de Segovia (1393-1458) was a prominent figure in the theological field[151]. He graduated in 1422 as a master in Theology, and afterwards, he lectured in the Chair of Bible and the Vespers Chair of Theology in Salamanca for ten years, before 1432. He participated in the sessions of the Council of Basel and he defended clearly conciliarist views. In 1434 he opposed to papal legates presiding the sessions: «The Council represents the Church, and the Pope is nothing but a most noble member of it». Back then he was a representative of the University of Salamanca, since 1433. For Segovia, all the Christians, even the Pope, had to yield to the authority of the Council. He wrote a *History of the Council of Basel* [*Historia del Concilio de Basilea*] in nineteen volumes. He started the work in 1450 and it was left unfinished, because he only wrote it until the year 1444. He was able to use the minutes of the Council for it. Juan Alfonso de Segovia donated his library to the University of Salamanca in 1457 but, by wish of the Pope Pius II, the most select parts of the work were sent to the Vatican Library[152].

There were other figures who had been educated in Salamanca and who defended postures in favor of the papacy. Rodrigo Sánchez de Arévalo (1404-1470), doctor in Law and bachelor in Theology by the University of Salamanca, was in Basel as a secretary of Alfonso García de Santamaría, better known as Alonso de Cartagena[153]. Sánchez de Arévalo's posture evolved from a moderate conciliarism to «an absolute defense of papal absolutism»[154]. Other men who had studied in Salamanca also intervened in defense of the papacy in some stages of the Council of Basel, such as the Catalan Cardinal Juan Casanova (+1436), the Cardinals Juan De Mella (+1467) and Juan de Carvajal (+1469). They became renowned in the fields of Diplomacy and Law. The Dominican Juan de Torquemada (1388-1468) had studied Theology in San Esteban, in Salamanca and he was a master by the University of Paris (1425). In 1417 he accompanied his Provincial Superior to the Council of Constance. In 1432 he arrived at Basel and he established a relation with the clear defenders of the papacy. He defended the monarchical nature of the Church, the full authority of the Pope and his power as a source of other ecclesiastical powers, and these views would grant him the purple in 1439[155].

With regard to the relation between Common law and Royal law in the context of that period in Salamanca, we have the methodological book of Juan Alfonso de Benavente, which was written around 1453. According to this work, the *Ordenamiento de Alcalá* was to be followed first, then the *Fuero Real*, followed by the *Partidas*, and failing all that, jurists could turn to Common law. This and other positions of jurists have led to diverse interpretations: full authority and priority of the Laws of the Kingdom; subordination of the Royal law to the Common, Roman-Canon law; or the coexistence of both systems in practice[156].

In the Faculty of Theology of Salamanca in the 15th century, the main authorities in the different subjects were Peter Lombard and his *Sentencias*, Nicholas of Lyra for biblical studies and Saint Bonaventure and Saint Thomas in the two Studia Generalia of mendicant friars in the city: Franciscans and Dominicans.

Alfonso Fernández de Madrigal (1401-1455), better known as *El Tostado* was a prominent theological figure of that time. He was a student in the College of San Bartolomé since 1433 and he was a Rector of that institution in 1437-1438. He was a master in Arts and Theology and an bachelor in Canon law[157]. He occupied the Chairs of Moral Philosophy, Poetics and Bible Studies

17. *Coat of arms of Alonso de Madrigal, El Tostado († 1455), on the
East façade of the Escuelas Mayores building.*

(1449) in the University, and he was a Maestrescuela there from 1446[158]. There are no references of him being present in the Council of Basel, although we know that he held moderate conciliarist views. He defended the infallibility of the Council with regard to matters of faith and customs. He travelled to Italy and he presented his theological thesis in a scholastic confrontation in Siena in 1443, while the pontifical Curia was present. The propositions he defended were judged by a court of cardinals and theologians and they were later discredited.

He was an expert on Latin, Greek and Hebrew, and he wrote about different theological, biblical and mythological-historiographical subjects. However, he stood out because of his biblical exegeses, with commentaries on almost all the books in the Old Testament, the Gospel according to Saint Matthew and the *Ecclesiastical History* of Eusebius of Caesarea. Actually, he had planned a great project with commentaries on the entire Bible, both in the literal sense and in the three spiritual senses (allegorical, tropological and anagogical)[159].

In contrast with the theological and scholastic controversies, the 15th century witnessed a strong trend that was based on the Scriptures as a supporting «corpus» for theological reflection. Followers of this school of thought were convinced that the Scriptures contained no mistakes, because they were directly inspired by the Holy Spirit and thus represented the safest possible source. El Tostado shared these ideas[160]. On the other hand, the relations with Jews in the Peninsula also favored the interest and rise in exegetic activity during this century.

In this context, we have to highlight El Tostado's leaning towards the literal sense of the Scriptures as the only valid method to reach firm theological conclusions[161]. He agreed in this regard with Saint Thomas Aquinas and the entire Thomist school, which underlines the importance of the literal interpretation in order to avoid subjectivity.

El Tostado presents «a character which is at the same time late medieval and pre-humanist»[162]. We are faced here with an Aristotelian-Thomist figure, with a formal mind and expressive style which is adapted to the academic patterns and conventions. However, his concern for moral Philosophy and the Classical authors lets us classify him as a pre-humanist[163]. This is the framework where his translations from Greek, his writings on mythological subjects and certain innovations in his scholastic lectures can be placed[164]. He offered some innovative contributions, such as his concern for textual criticism, his linguistic and etymological resources, the importance he granted to Aristotle and Saint Thomas Aquinas, his conciliarist stand and the criticism to the society and the Church of his time. The exegesis of El Tostado also presents a practical concern as a response to specific problems of his era, in contrast to speculative and logical-philosophical subtleties[165].

In Medicine, since the beginning of the 14th century, Avicenna's *Canon* becomes a staple in universities such as Montpellier. It was an Islamic coursebook that offered a rational systematization of the medical tradition of Hippocrates and Galen. During the 15th century, the Avicennist School was preponderant in the European universities. In Salamanca, the 3rd Constitution of 1411 already mentions Avicenna and Arnaldus de Villa Nova as some authors worthy of appearing in the planned Library of Authorities[166]. We can also notice, all along the 15th century, a repeated absenteeism of the incumbents of Chairs of Medicine in Salamanca, who were at the service of the royal courts and left teaching in charge of their substitutes[167].

With regard to Humanities, we can say that Castile was a recipient of the Italian classical and humanist tradition since the reign of Juan II in the cultured and court circles. That humanism was directed by the royal court and the ecclesiastics were in charge of its doctrine. However, the Italian «republicanism» conflicted with the Spanish historical memory and with its myths of the Goths, the Reconquista and the Monarchy. At the same time, the spread of the vernacular language[168] restricted the spread of Latin as a language of culture. Many of the most important intellectuals in these circles had studied in Salamanca[169].

In its first two centuries, the University of Salamanca did not have a library, strictly speaking. It is true that

Alfonso X had established a position of library clerk, but this was not a proper librarian, but some sort of bookseller who lent the books divided in offprints or individual *pecias* or pieces for copying. Some of these pieces of books were used as texts for the lectures[170]. The Pope Benedict XIII officially established a library in the 4th Constitution of 1411. The donation of books of Juan de Segovia to the University in 1457 was limited, and most of them ended up in the Vatican Library of Rome; some of them in the collegiate church of Valladolid and the Mercedarian monastery of that same city[171]. The Archbishop Diego de Anaya amassed a large collection of manuscripts on his travel to the Council of Constance and his later return via Bologna, and afterwards he donated these books to the College of San Bartolomé of Salamanca[172]. There are also references to some private libraries[173], and to manuscript shops, such as the ones in Desafiadero Street, next to the University, in 1383, one of which was run by a Jewish woman[174].

The evolution of the University in these years is still related to different environments, spaces and people from the Cathedral[175]. The Chapel of Santa Catalina was under construction in 1392. The Chapel of San Bartolomé was founded in 1422 for the burial of Diego de Anaya Maldonado. Meanwhile, between 1415 and 1433, the buildings of the Escuelas Mayores had been erected[176], with a Chapel dedicated to Saint Jerome[177]. However, this first building underwent consecutive remodeling because it was probably a group of Mudejar rooms made with masonry and bricks. It seems that while El Tostado was the Maestrescuela of the University (1446-1454), he enclosed the Escuelas and reconstructed some halls or classrooms[178]. The core buildings of the College of San Bartolomé were raised between 1413 and 1418. It was a construction of brick and plastered masonry which underwent some extensions along the 15th century[179].

3

THE SECOND HALF OF THE 15ᵀᴴ CENTURY AND THE ROYAL INTERVENTION

3.1. The Monarchs as patrons

IN THE MIDDLE OF THE 15TH CENTURY, the prestige of the University of Salamanca was recognized by the Cortes and the Kingdom[180]. The relation with the Kings is also properly established. In the first book of minutes of the Senate meetings that we have, from 1464, we can find an oath of loyalty from the University to Henry IV. In the conflict for succession between Joanna *la Beltraneja* and Isabella I of Castile, the noble houses in Salamanca took sides, and the group of Santo Tomé supported the daughter of Henry IV[181]. In March 1475, amidst the stormy clouds of the incoming Civil War, the University swears an oath of obeisance and loyalty to the Catholic Monarchs[182]. Isabella I and Ferdinand II confirmed all the privileges of the University and tried to defend the corporation against the interference of the citizens of Salamanca in the post elections or the assignment of Chairs. The Monarchs were mainly interested in the university training of jurists and physicians to fulfill the needs of the Kingdom[183]; and the Cortes of Toledo in 1480 promoted a larger role for men of letters in the government boards and the courts of justice[184]. The Popes maintain their connections with the University as well[185].

The Monarchs started to intervene in the University corporation by means of their visitors. In 1479 there was a schism between two conflicting Rectors. The Monarchs

[57]

18. *Minute book of University Senate meetings 1464-1474.*

interceded and ordered Doctor Tello de Buendía, scholar from San Bartolomé and Archdeacon of Toledo, to solve the conflict: A new Rector was chosen, albeit not completely according to the Constitutions. The clash spread from November 1479 to March 1480[186]. The conclusion seems to be that the different Rectors could become the leaders of University and of citizen factions. However, towards 1485, the Catholic Monarchs doubted their own prerogatives to send Royal visitors to the Studium without an authorization from the Pope[187]. In this regard, a bull by Alexander VI from August 1497 that was sent at the request of the Monarchs entrusted Cisneros, Archbishop of Toledo, and Deza, Bishop of Salamanca, with visiting the Studia Generalia and the private schools of the Kingdom, including the University of Salamanca. There are no records of the visit ever taking place, but the bull bears witness of the ambiguity of the Royal patronage over the University, because it seems that the Monarchs did not dare to send visitors directly[188].

The Catholic Monarchs started to control the appointment of the Maestrescuela, citing their rights of appointment and patronage over the University and the Church in their Kingdoms. In 1477 there was a conflict in the election. The academic Senate appointed Pascual Ruiz de Aranda; but the Monarchs, on their part, had obtained from the Pope Sixtus IV the position of Maestrescuela for Gutierre Álvarez de Toledo, son of the Duke of Alba. The Pope supported the King and Queen, against the protests of the University.

The jurisdiction of the Maestrescuela clashed with that of the judges who depended on the Bishop and the Archbishop of Santiago. The Catholic Monarchs were in favor of increasing the power of the scholastic authority by granting him a large jurisdictional authority without the interference of lay courts, and by ratifying the privileges of the conservatory bulls and the papal Constitutions: Capitulations of Santa Fe, May 17th 1492. With regard to the territorial competences, the authority of the Maestrescuela as an ordinary judge reached the entire Christendom or the territories of the Kindgom, depending on the jurisdiction upon which he was acting, ecclesiastical or Royal[189]. His geographical boundaries for bringing the defendants to justice were defined by a radius of four *dietas* around the town of Salamanca in 1492; and finally to only 2 *dietas* in 1494. Each *dieta* represented a distance of ten leagues[190]. However, these limits were crossed in several occasions due to the exceptional nature of some cases. The Maestrescuela was an ordinary judge, with *mero et mixto imperio* (authority over the criminal and civil law), who was in charge of all the disputes related with the University. The only superiors he had and recognized were the Pope or the King.

3.2. Institutional and power aspects

All along the 15th century, the high-ranking members and nobles from the main houses and families of the town meddled in the appointment of posts and positions and in the designation of Chairs with bribes and threats. There are several testimonies and protests of the University before the Royal Council, in April 1431 or May 1480, for example[191]. However, at the same time, both lecturers and students were involved (of their own free will or not) in the clashes between the different factions of the town[192]. Sometimes, this situation led even to classes coming to a halt[193].

With regard to the institutional aspects, there are several government boards in the second half of the 15th century, when we have documentation of the Senate meetings from 1464[194]. We can observe that the general corporate assembly from the origins of the institution has lost its importance.

The board of the Rector and his counselors elected the Rector, counselors, beadle, syndic, library clerk, and estate assessors. This organism also managed the vacant Chairs, absence of lecturers and fines, classroom allocation, and was in charge of different aspects regarding teaching, lectures, etc. There already are references to the existence of gifts, bribes and armed coercion over the voters for the Chairs. In case of disagreement, the papal Constitutions applied.

The academic Senate is in charge of the economic and estate matters, as well as salaries, repairs and building work. In this age, representatives are elected by co-optation, like the board of the Rector and his counselors[195]. In spite of what was established in the Constitutions, the documents do not clearly reveal the supremacy of this organism over the board of the Rector and the counselors.

The board of professors or doctors, presided by the primicerius, controls the questions of the remainders and the payment of professors, celebrations, etc.

There are other boards or meetings with vague borders: sometimes, counselors and representatives came together, sometimes with the presence of professors; sometimes the professors met alone. The organization does not seem to be systematic, but adapted to the circumstances.

The Senate meetings with the presence of the Rector, professors, representatives and counselors dealt with extraordinary matters, such as the preparation of regulations and statutes. They were referred to as «plenary meetings» in the 16th century, when they were completely consolidated after including the representation of the temporary and non-tenured professors who appeared all along the 15th century.

In these institutional and power aspects, the relations between the University and the Cathedral are particularly interesting. In the second half of the 15th century there are references to the existence of families and networks of influence intertwined in both institutions[196]: That is the case of the family of the Bishop Gonzalo de Vivero or the Maestrescuela Juan Ruiz de Camargo[197]. These people had the ability to advance in their careers in the positions of the Cathedral chapter and the University corporation at the same time. We can find Rectors and Vice-rectors, representatives and professors who are at the same time Prebendaries. There is also a certain progressive «scale» in the academic posts, which means that we must not imagine a University government too open to young students with no connections or resources[198]. Between 1464 and 1481, eight canonists with a degree were Rectors: three were doctors, one was a graduate and four were bachelors; which rather puts into question the idea of a rectorship of «simple students»[199].

Around the decade of 1460, the University Archive is enriched[200] and the minute books of the Senate meetings first appear, we can draw an outline of the existing Chairs. In Law there are two Prime Chairs of Canons, and one of Decrees, two Vespers Chairs of Canons, one of Sext and Clementinae. Six in total. The Prime Chair is valued at 272 florins, the Chair of Decrees is valued in 204 florins, the Vespers Chair in 150 florins and the Sixt Chair in 150 florins too. Also, from this time we start to know the name of some bachelors who occupied the temporary Chairs of Canons[201], although their numbers are not clear[202].

In that same decade, there is a Prime Chair of Theology with a salary of 150 florins, a Vespers Chair with 113 florins and a Bible Chair with 100 florins[203]. In Medicine there is a Prime Chair with 150 florins and a Vespers Chair with 113 florins[204]. In Arts/Philosophy, there is a Chair of Moral Philosophy with a salary of 100 florins, a Chair of Natural Philosophy with 100 florins, a Chair of *Logica magna* with 100 florins and a last Chair of Summulae with 100 florins[205]. In Medicine and Logic there are temporary Chairs as well[206]. In Grammar there are two Prime Chairs with a salary of 100 florins each, one Chair of Rhetoric with 60 florins and several temporary teaching positions which are not clearly defined[207]. Finally, the Chair of Languages (Hebrew, Chaldean and Arabic) had a salary of 100 florins, and the Chairs of Astrology and Music received 60 florins each[208]. That is, there were 25 Chairs in total in Salamanca during the decade of 1460.

In the field of Humanities or Grammar there was a difference between the bachelors in charge of teaching for one year (*bachilleres de Gramática*) and the subordinates who merely «repeated» the lessons. This last group of subordinates was in charge of the starting students, and they could be «provided by the University» or they could work as private teachers at home, without an official appointment. The salaries of all these Grammar bachelors and subordinates were paid directly by the students[209].

This entire situation leads us to the problem of salaries in the temporary or standing Chairs. It seems that those in charge of these Chairs in the main faculties, who were mainly bachelors, did not earn any salary until 1439. In that date, some bonuses were established[210]. On the other hand, custom dictated that bachelors and those in charge of repeating the lessons were paid thanks to collections among the students, as was the case in Bologna and other Universities. These collections still existed in the second half of the 15th century, but they were cancelled in 1480[211], and the associated expenses were transferred to the coffers of the University.

Normally, bachelors, graduates and doctors took the examinations for paid Chairs, with frequent confrontations and briberies[212]. However, in 1489, Pope Innocent VIII ordered that in those examinations, those with the highest academic rank were given precedence, except for the Chairs of Grammar, Music, Logic, Rhetoric and Astronomy[213].

With regard to bachelors, the 17th Constitution of Martin V was still in force in 1478. It stated that bachelors could read lectures in the University buildings or outside them. In December of that same year, the board of the Rector and his counselors was still in charge of granting licenses to teach «in exchange for money or not» in the buildings of the Escuelas or in private houses. In this last case, lessons in private houses must not coincide with others of the same nature and at the same time in the public buildings of the University[214].

The temporary Chairs (those that only lasted for one year) and Chairs occupied by substitutes may have been regulated and consolidated as permanent posts between 1480 and 1502[215], with their respective salaries. At first, these consolidated yearly Chairs were assigned by votes from the students, but since the academic year of 1504-1505 it was agreed that the Senate would appoint them, in order to prevent restlessness and fights between the students[216].

In line with these consolidated Chairs, bachelors still abided by the Constitutional legislation that established that they had to teach lectures for some years. The academic year was usually reduced to only a few months, with

19. *Chest with five keys in the Room of Manuscripts of the General Historical Library, 15th century.*

two or three lessons per week before a group of friends. Although their merits stated that they were «professors», they actually were not; and this name must be limited to those with tenured Chairs and to those who had taken and passed an examination and earned a salary[217].

With regard to the teaching aspects of the Cathedral of Salamanca, in 1474, the Pope Sixtus IV, by request of the Bishops and the Cathedral chapter of Castile, granted two positions of Canons in his Cathedrals: One Canonry for a magister and theologian to assist with the preaching and a legal Canonry for a jurist to teach Canon law. They were chosen by the Cathedral chapters but, sometimes, the Pontiffs appointed them[218]. Gonzalo de Vivero, Bishop of Salamanca between 1447 and 1482, showed a clear intellectual inclination. To his knowledge of legal matters he added an interest for Astronomy and other subjects.

Although the teaching aspects of the University were regulated by the Constitutions of 1422, all along the 15th century some decisions were taken in the Senate with regard to the teaching of Dialectics (1444) or Ethics (1466)[219], for example.

In the Cortes of Toledo in 1480, the Catholic Monarchs commanded a revision of the method of appointment of degrees that were granted «via apostolic letters» in the University[220]. This was a system of papal appointment that dated from the time of Martin V, with an easier exam and no expenses, to which the University objected. Innocent VIII admitted in 1487 that graduates who had obtained their degrees with this system should not enjoy the honors, privileges and liberties of doctors and masters who graduated through the University[221]. Students from the College of San Bartolomé, on the basis of their humble position, convinced the Popes to let them take their graduation exams with reduced fees. This privilege was granted in 1469 and ratified in 1491.

Among other regulations, the Catholic Monarchs established the *Protomedicato*, a tribunal of physicians which, under the authority of the Monarchs, controlled the University Degrees of Medicine and Surgery in 1494.

In Salamanca in the 15th century there is a predominance of Law students, particularly canonists, and also an important contingent of clergymen[222]. The number of registered students ranged from around 600 at the beginning of the century and almost 3,000 at the end[223]. Other authors estimate that the number was around 1,000 students in a town of around 15,000 people well into the 15th century[224]. Sometimes, epidemics and famine had an influence on the number of registered students and the cancellation of the lessons, as happened in 1479[225].

The students came mainly from Old and New Castile, León and Portugal, because the Crown of Aragón was more inclined towards the south of France and Italy. In general terms, the teaching staff of Salamanca in the 15th century also came from the peninsular Kingdoms of Castile, León and Portugal. One of the first foreigners at that time was the Italian Nicolo Antonio, who taught Poetry in the years 1465-1467[226].

With regard to the halls of residence, monasteries and institutions associated with the University, we know that the Constitutions of the College of San Bartolomé were reformed in 1469[227]. This College received in 1491 a renewal of the grant to graduate with reduced costs[228]. Previously, in 1479, the University had unsuccessfully tried to make Cardinal Mendoza found a new College in Salamanca which would from 1494 become the College of Santa Cruz, in Valladolid[229]. The Halls of Pan y Carbón received a privilege in 1501 by which its students could remain in the Halls after graduating[230]. In this time of the Catholic Monarchs, the importance of the College of San Bartolomé in the education of the administrative ranks of the Church and the Kingdom is outstanding: we can find alumni from the College in the Royal Council, the Council of the Inquisition, the Chancelleries of Valladolid and Granada and several Bishoprics[231]. On the other hand, the statute of the town of Toledo from 1449 which excluded converts from Judaism or New Christians from public office had a great impact in Castile. It inspired a new statute in the College of San Bartolomé which stated that descendants from Jews could not become chaplains or scholars. That statute dated from the middle of the 15th century, and it was ratified and expanded in 1505[232].

3.4. INTELLECTUAL ATMOSPHERE

There are some authors who interpret the University of Salamanca of the 15th century as a basically medieval institution which preceded the Renaissance Humanism of the end of the century. Jurists, in particular, were comfortable inside the system of the medieval Common Roman-Canon law[233]. Moreover, there are only a few works from University jurists in the first half of the 15th century, not because they did not survive until our time, but because these jurists did not write much, as their contemporary Alonso de Cartagena points out.

However, some canonists did produce some written works and they were mutual disciples or masters. Juan Alfonso de Benavente (+1477)[234] was a master to his son, Diego Alfonso. He, in turn, was a master to Juan de Castilla. Gonzalo García de Villadiego succeeded Diego Gómez de Zamora in his Chair, and he was a master to Juan López de Palacios Rubios. Among these masters there are certain methodological and doctrinal constants[235]. In the manuscripts that we have from these authors, scattered over different libraries in Spain and abroad, we can find repetitions, treatises and commentaries, speeches requesting degrees, etc.

Since the time of the Catholic Monarchs, jurists found a clear support from the Monarchy and their works were spread thanks to the printing press. This resulted in the diffusion of some names, such as Gonzalo García de Villadiego, Juan López de Segovia, Diego de Segura, Rodrigo Suárez and Juan López de Palacios Rubios; some of them even at a European level[236].

In this stage, the Catholic Monarchs continued with the traditional Italian methods for teaching Law, «those of the gloss and the commentary of texts and authorities, with an emphasis on practice», without a real concern for humanist critique, the purity of Latin text and the establishment of an historical context. And this is the framework in which we have to analyze the objections presented by the grammarian Elio Antonio de Nebrija[237].

Although university teaching in Salamanca was based on the Roman-Canon corpus, references to the laws of the Kingdom were not overlooked either. This can be seen in the writings of several lecturers, or in the collection of the library of the Cathedral chapter, according to the registers from 1533. They show the pontifical and Justinian works compilations, together with glossators and commentators; but we can also find the works of jurists from Castile, such as Rodrigo Sánchez de Arévalo, Juan Alfonso de Benavente, Palacios Rubios, Juan de Castilla, Montalvo, and the texts of Kingdom Law itself, with or without glosses[239].

Most of the jurists from Salamanca at that time supported the full authority of the Monarch «above the positive law, with the capacity to promulgate laws, interpret, abrogate and dismiss them». In this trend we can find Montalvo, García de Villadiego and Palacios Rubios, and we might even include Rodrigo Suárez and Diego del Castillo too[239].

Among the different jurists who were connected with Salamanca in the time of the Catholic Monarchs, the specialized authors point out some names[240], such as Alonso Díaz de Montalvo, canonist and civilist, who was a student in Salamanca and Lérida. He was at the service of different Kings in courts and tribunals. One of his best known works were the *Royal Orders* [*Ordenanzas reales*], a compilation of the laws of Castile.

Also, Rodrigo Suárez, bachelor in Laws by the University of Salamanca, who was a substitute professor in the years 1474-1475 and a member judge of the Chancellery of Valladolid

For his part, Juan López de Palacios Rubios was a student in the College of San Bartolomé, graduate in Canons by the University of Salamanca and doctor and

20. *Juan Alfonso de Benavente*, Compilatio decretorum moralium praedicatoribus et confesoribus, *15th century.*

professor in the Prime Chair of Canons in Valladolid. He was a judge, president of the Council of the Mesta and member of the Council of Castile. Among his works there is a commentary to the Laws of Toro.

Finally, Lorenzo Galíndez de Carvajal, professor in the Prime Chair of Laws in the University of Salamanca (1503-1527) was a member of the Council of Castile. He received a good legal education and he was an outstanding writer of commissioned royal chronicles and annals; and of some studies on lineages and majorats.

21. *Central medallion in the first story of the façade of the University, with the effigies of the Catholic Monarchs.*

The theological orthodoxy of Salamanca in the 15th century was interrupted by the doctrine of Pedro Martínez de Osma (c. 1430-1480) on the subject of penance. He was a scholar in the College of San Bartolomé since 1444, and he was a professor in the Prime Chair of Theology from 1463 to 1478. Towards 1476, he published his book *De confessione*. He got ahead of the Lutheran theories on confession and indulgences. Among other theses, he defends that the forgiveness of sins and the remission of temporary penance derive only from contrition, in a process that takes place between man and God, without the intervention of the Church. He was condemned by the Cortes of Zaragoza (1478) and by a synod of the Archbishop of Toledo in Alcalá (1479)[241]. Osma's books were publicly burned in the Escuelas Mayores after a Mass of the Holy Spirit on June 15th 1479[242].

With regard to the theological aspects themselves, Osma's book *In Simbolum quicumque* shows the importance he grants to the *Summa Theologica*, by Saint Thomas Aquinas, who is the most cited authority of the work[243]. And all these quotes and references are continued in other of his works. In this sense, Pedro de Osma is a precursor in Salamanca of the defense and establishment of Thomism, a theory that would afterwards be followed by Diego de Deza and Francisco de Vitoria[244]. Contrary to Duns Scotus and the Subtle Doctors, he proposed a return to the sources, the Bible, the Patristics and the Councils[245]. He was obviously an expert on biblical hermeneutics[246].

In Medicine we can observe real dynasties. Fernán Álvarez Malla, the first doctor of the Queen, was a professor in the Prime Chair of Medicine between 1445 and 1469. His son, Gabriel Álvarez Abarca, second doctor of the Queen, occupied the Chair from 1475 to 1496. Since 1486-1487 he comes under the personal service of the Catholic Monarchs and effectively abandons teaching. He is replaced in the Chair by his brother Fernán Álvarez Abarca from 1496 to 1526[247].

Apart from the authorities of Avicenna, Hippocrates and Galen, the medical training was associated with the Chair of Astrology, due to the problems related to the physical constitution and the astral influences. There were also links to the Chair of Natural Philosophy, occupied by Master Antón Rodríguez de Salamanca since 1479[248]. Among the purchases for the Library in those years there are references to books by authors such as Constantine the African and Galen[249].

With regard to the Arts, nominalism in Castile spread mainly through Alcalá. Salamanca was an essentially

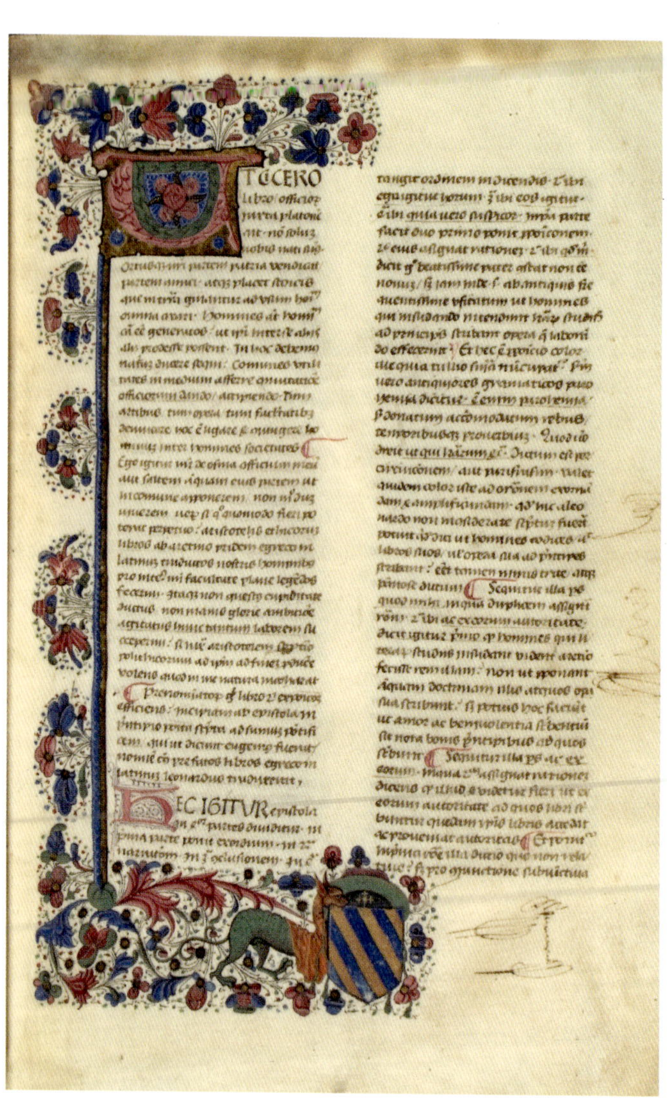

22. *Pedro Martínez de Osma,* Commentaria in Ethicorum Aristotelis libros, *15th century.*

realist institution in the 15th century, with the exception of the arguments on nominalism between Pedro Martínez de Osma and the Franciscan Pedro de Caloca[250]. Osma, to whom we have referred before, goes beyond the nominalist conceptualism of his first years to Aristotelian realism. He occupied the Chair of Moral Philosophy from 1457 to 1463. In his commentaries to Aristotle's *Ethics*, *Politics* and *Metaphysics*, he comes closer to the philosopher, who had been rehabilitated by Bruni in his *Vita Aristotelis*, against the scholastic interpretation[251]. Osma shows humanist concerns when he deals with grammatical problems and appreciates Rhetoric against the subtle abstractions and the affected verbosity of the nominalist Dialectics[252]. With his wide learning, Osma was also an innovator, and he probably was one of the first university teachers who edited their works in a printing press[253].

The Chair of Astrology-Mathematics regained its vitality in Salamanca since the middle of the 15th century[254]. From that moment we know the sequence of its main professors: Nicolás Polonio (-1464), Juan de Salaya (1464-1469), Diego de Calzadilla (1467-1475), Fernando de Fontiveros (1476-1481), Diego de Torres (1481-1496) and Rodrigo Basurto (1496-1504)[255]. Some of them were connected to the College of San Bartolomé[256], and they formed a scientific school of a certain importance, especially in the creation of astronomic charts applied to navigation[257].

Another important figure was the Jew Abraham Zacut, from Salamanca, who was not strictly speaking a professor. He finished one of the most important Astronomy texts of his century towards 1478: *Hibbur (The Great Compilation)*. The text is accompanied by some tables which were greatly relevant and useful in that time[258].

This astronomic school also had an influence on the great vault of stars painted by Fernando Gallego between 1483 and 1486 in the Library, which some authors have interpreted as a true educational planetary[259]. Also, the masters in this school were consulted in some important occasions. For example, in the ambiguous case of

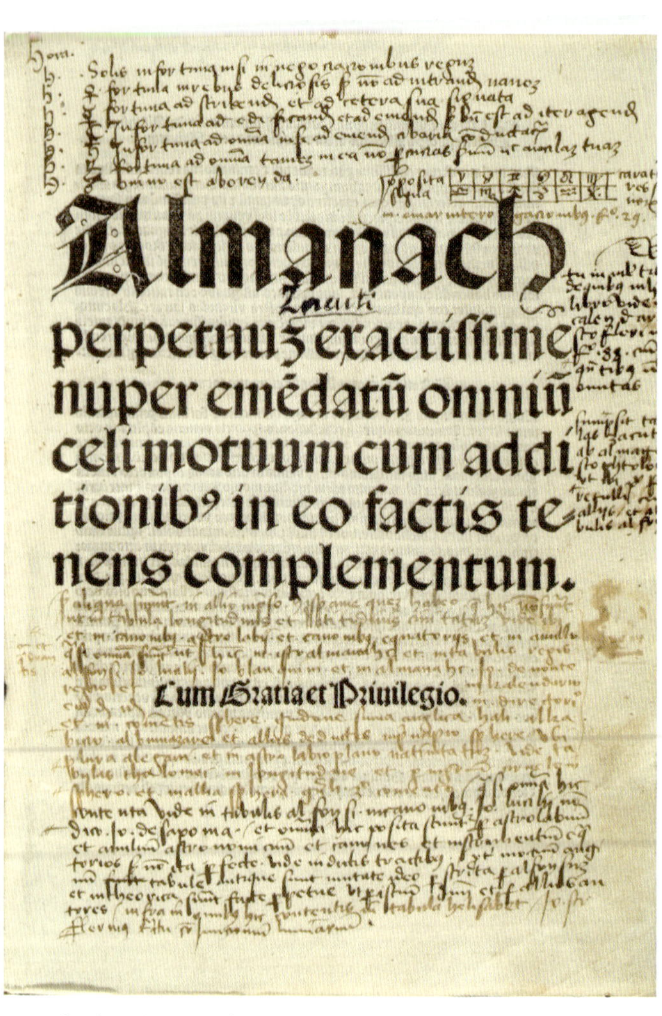

23. *Abraham Zacut*, Almanach perpetuum, *Venice, 1502.*

Christopher Columbus[260]. For his part, Diego de Torres, student in San Bartolomé and professor of Astrology from 1481 to 1496, was sent as an advisor to the Catholic Monarchs in 1494 on the occasion of the Treaty of Tordesillas between the Crowns of Castile and Portugal in which they demarcated their maritime territories. On the other hand, Ptolemy's *Geography* started a progressive change in cosmographic view of the world by the University from 1498 to 1530[261].

Elio Antonio de Nebrija (1442-1522) studied in Salamanca from 1457 to 1463. His masters were Pedro Martínez de Osma, Ruiz de Aranda and Nicolás Polonio. He spent ten years in Italy. In 1476 he obtained the Prime Chair of Grammar in Salamanca until 1488, and he also taught Rhetoric. He left the Chair and the University to work for Juan de Zúñiga, Master of Alcántara. He went back to Salamanca in 1503 and occupied the same Chair as before; and left it on that same year to become a Royal Chronicler. In 1505 he returned to his post until 1508, when he took the examinations for the Chair of Rhetoric. In 1513, he failed in a new examination for the Prime Chair of Grammar and moved to the University of Alcalá[262].

For humanists such as Nebrija[263], Grammar is the basis of all other knowledge, because it gives access to the original language in which they were created. This involved a critical position regarding the translation of the *Vulgate* by the theologians or the lack of knowledge of Classical Latin of commentators of Roman law such as Accursius. For these humanists, the importance lied in the terminological analysis, the history of words and their use. They look for examples of good language and they apply them to different spheres: legal, theological, philosophical or scientific[264]. Grammar claims its place as an arbitrator of knowledge, based on Classical Latin, historical philology and textual criticism[265].

Greek studies started with Arias Barbosa (c. 1465-1540), who appears in the registers as a permanent professor towards 1495[266]. Together with Hernán Núñez de Guzmán, *El Pinciano*, he would later become one of the purest humanists in the field of textual criticism[267].

In conclusion, apart from legal studies in the Italian tradition, we can establish two innovative intellectual trends in Salamanca in the 15th century: the scholastic and Thomist line in Theology and the school of philological humanism. A third trend, the nominalist approach to the Arts, would not become established until well into the next century with the initiative of Juan Martínez Silíceo[268].

A printing press was installed in Salamanca around the year 1472[269]. However, important books of the University were bought in the international European presses; as was established in the Cortes of Toledo on May 1480, which paved the way for the purchase of those works. Medina del Campo appears as a hub for the book market in Castile all along the 15th century[270].

24. *Paintings on the vault of the old Library of the University of Salamanca, between 1483 and 1486, attributed to Fernando Gallego.*

One of the oldest references to the University Library can be found in the administrative Archives and dates back to 1465[271]. In this date, the Constitutions and privileges of the University are copied to be stored in it[272]. Back then,

25. *Gothic entrance of the Hospital of the Studium —currently the Rector's office—, whose works started in 1472.*

the Library consisted of a series of benches and books tied up in chains. It had to be opened two hours after the Prime lessons and one hour and a half after three o'clock in the afternoon (Vespers). In the year 1471 there were 201 volumes in the Library[273]. Also, there are evidences of a certain coming and going of book copyists[274]. Afterwards, there were important donations to the Library by the Maestrescuela Juan Ruiz de Camargo in 1477 and Doctor Alonso Ortiz, Canon of Toledo, in 1507/1508[275]. The University Library could be completed with that of the College of San Bartolomé, which existed since the time of Anaya, and with those of the Cathedral and some monasteries. The Cathedral Library was made richer with the contributions of the Bishops Gonzalo de Vivero in 1480 and Juan de Castilla in 1510, both of whom were students in the University. And, to properly install the Library, the Cathedral chapter agreed in 1484 to rebuild and fit out the Chapel of Santa Catalina[276]. For its part, in 1489, the Dominican chapter of Salamanca insisted on the necessity of having well-equipped libraries in the monasteries of the Order[277].

The buildings of the University underwent some remodeling in this period. The Hospital of the Studium, for example, was rebuilt from 1472[278], when Juan Ruiz de Camargo was the Maestrescuela. Around 1473, the works of the Library of the Studium were approved, and it was built on the site of the old Chapel. Moorish builders were employed and the vault was closed in September 1479[279]. From 1483, this vault was decorated with astronomical paintings, attributed to Fernando Gallego[280]. There are different opinions regarding the ideology behind the iconographic plan of the paintings[281]. In this period, we also have descriptions of the Chapel being used as a meeting hall[282].

4

THE KINGS ASSERT THEIR
AUTHORITY OVER THE PONTIFFS

4.1. ROYAL VISITORS

FOR SOME AUTHORS, the Studium of Salamanca kept its ecclesiastical and corporative autonomy from the Catholic Monarchs[283]. In 1504, some months before the death of Queen Isabella, and in view of the disturbances that had taken place in the University, the Council of Castile asked for the passing of a rule that stated that students could only own one sword[284]. The University resisted and argued that students could not be left defenseless against the inhabitants of the town.

In 1512, the Catholic King sent Diego Ramírez de Villaescusa, Bishop of Málaga and alumnus of the College of San Bartolomé, as a visitor to Salamanca. This visit was not gladly accepted by the Senate of the University, and there were signs of a certain corporative resistance against the royal attempts at imposing their control. However, some of the statutes and regulations were discussed. For example, Villaescusa tried to strengthen the authority of the Rector, and he proposed that whoever occupied that position had to be a graduate and commit to a three-year term. Also, a proposal was discussed about a possible system of non-tenured Chairs, contrary to what was established in the Constitutions of 1422. There were even talks on the possibility that all students were confined into the Halls, or that a prelate from the Kingdom controlled the activities of the Maestrescuela. It looks as if the visitor tried to establish a hierarchical concentration of powers, maybe in order to come closer to the model offered by the recently founded University of Alcalá, which followed the Paris example of institutional eclecticism. Let us remember that the Constitutions proposed by Francisco Jiménez de Cisneros were finished in January 1510. In any case, the Senate of the corporation confronted the visitor. They argued that they were an ecclesiastical community with papal Constitutions and privileges that were guarded by the Maestrescuela[285], and they put into question the royal authority to visit and intervene in the University. On the contrary, the Bishop of Málaga argued that the Monarchs had been patrons of the Studium and tried to impose his reformist authority. This led to a cut and thrust in which the intentions of the visitor were ultimately thwarted[286].

The influence of the Pontiffs at the beginning of the 16th century can be seen in a bull of December 1518 which clarified some doubts of the University with regard to the Constitutions of 1422. The bull focused on the clause that banned people from Salamanca, those who had been living in the town for at least ten years without being associated with the University, and relatives of noblemen and the rich from becoming Rectors or counselors. The rule tried to prevent members of powerful families from occupying positions in the government of the University, which would diminish the freedom and independence of the Studium. The consultation had been motivated by the election of Luis de Pimentel as a Rector in the academic year 1511-1512. De Pimentel was a member of the family of the Counts of Benavente, and he had powerful relatives in the town of Salamanca[287].

The bull of Pope Adrian VI in 1522 also shows the strength of the pontifical connections. The bull reduced the requirements to obtain an bachelor in Canons and Laws established in the Constitutions of 1422 to five years of study and practice[288].

In 1529, Charles V sent two visitors, Pedro Pacheco, Dean of Santiago; and the graduate Alonso Mexía, a Canon from Toledo; who deposed and exiled the Rector Pedro García Lagasca, against the wishes of the University. They also forced the passing of some regulations that excluded certain scholars from the University government, mainly Canons from the Cathedral[289] and chaplains of different churches: it seems that they were part of an oligarchy that had gained control of the University in the last years. The visitors imposed Hernán Pérez de Oliva as a new Rector and they promoted the creation of new statutes,

26. *Cloister of the wells in the Monastery of San Esteban in Salamanca (1500-1510), closely related to the Faculty of Theology from the beginning of the 15th century.*

which were not to the liking of the Senate and were not accepted. It appears as this was a ploy from the members of the Colleges to establish a Rector administration made up of collegiate members, and there were some groups who were opposed to this measure. In any case, the references show confusion, a diversity of regulations and blurred rules[290]. We still have a rough book or working paper, some sort of unfinished draft that was not fully reviewed in the meeting, which gave rise to discrepancies and did not receive the final approval of the Council or the Apostolic See. The deliberations regarding some of these regulations went on through the minute books of meetings of the years 1530-1532[291].

In autumn 1538, Juan de Córdoba, Abbot of Villanueva de Rute, came to visit. A delegation from the University met the visitor and structured an entire corpus of statutes that would be approved by the whole Senate afterwards. It seems that this visit marks the end of a whole process of legal fermentation which started on the previous decade, and there are some references of earlier drafts, such as the one from 1529. The final result were the Statutes of 1538, which were grouped into 65 titles, albeit with a certain disorder. The sections on the academic authorities follow what was established in the Constitutions of 1422, and the importance of the plenary meetings of the staff is strengthened. There is a new regulation on faculties, lectures, authors and subjects, and on the competitive examinations as well. There are also new economic regulations or norms regarding board and lodging of students. As we have just pointed out, the University corporation approved these statutes and had them printed. With this measure, the University got ahead of the bull of Pope Paul III from 1543, which granted the University the privilege of reforming the Constitutions with the consent of two thirds of the plenary meeting of the staff[292]. This is one of the last appearances of the pontifical authority in the University sphere[293]. From this moment, the medieval Constitutions coexisted with the newly approved Statutes[294].

27. *Statue of Saint Augustine, created by Felipe Bigarny. This figure comes from the old altarpiece of the Chapel, 1503-1504.*

With regard to the institutional aspects, the so called plenary meeting of the staff becomes consolidated at the beginning of the 16th century, together with the three government groups recognized in the medieval papal Constitutions (Rector and counselors, representatives and professors/doctors), and it is clearly defined in the decade of 1530: it was made up of the union of the board of counselors, the Senate and the doctors of the Studium, together with the Rector and the Maestrescuela[295].

In the economic area, the income of the University grows. Between 1518 and 1538, we find a favorable climate with a surplus for the institutions. The income in the decade of 1520-1530 ranged between 2,500,000 and 5,000,000 maravedís, with a growing trend[296], and this material wealth would undoubtedly contribute to the expansion of the Renaissance in Salamanca.

Different halls of residence and monasteries joined the University of Salamanca in the first half of the 16th century. In 1504, the Priory of San Vicente, in Salamanca, became a hall of residence[297]. In 1523, the Pope authorized the foundation of the College of Cuenca[298]; and in 1525 he authorized the creation of the Fonseca College[299].

These new times would also have their plastic representation. In March 1509, the construction of a new Library had started on the west side of the Escuelas Mayores, which increased the height of the Chapel and its decorations[300]. And from the decade of 1540, the University of Salamanca consolidated its new journey under the direct supervision of the Monarchs. The corporative autonomy and the pontifical references drifted apart gradually. The symbol of this change in the situation is the new plateresque façade, which was erected in the decade of 1520[301] to glorify the Emperor Charles[302]. The construction is a daydream of the Imperial Rome and the Hispanic Monarchy[303].

5
REFERENCES

AGUADÉ NIETO, Santiago (coord.), *Universidad, cultura y sociedad en la Edad Media*, Alcalá, Universidad de Alcalá, 1994.

ALFONSO DE BENAVENTE, Juan, *Ars et Doctrina Studendi et Docendi*. Critical edition by Bernardo Alonso Rodríguez, Salamanca, Universidad Pontificia, 1972.

ALONSO RODRÍGUEZ, Bernardo, *Juan Alfonso de Benavente. Canonista salmantino del siglo XV*, Roma/Madrid, CSIC, 1964.

ALONSO RODRÍGUEZ, Bernardo, «En torno a los canonistas medievales salmantinos», *Proceedings of the Fifth International Congress of Medieval Canon Law, Salamanca, 1976*, Roma Città del Vaticano, 1980.

ALONSO RODRÍGUEZ, Bernardo, «Las Escuelas de Cánones del Estudio salmantino en la Edad Media», in *Actas I Congreso de Historia de Salamanca*, I, Salamanca, Diputación de Salamanca, 1992, pp. 461-476.

ALONSO ROMERO, Mª Paz, *Universidad y sociedad corporativa. Historia del privilegio jurisdiccional del Estudio salmantino*, Madrid, Tecnos, 1997.

ALONSO ROMERO, Mª Paz, «Las Constituciones medievales», in *Historia de la Universidad de Salamanca. II. Estructuras y flujos*, Salamanca, Ediciones Universidad de Salamanca, 2004, pp. 93-108.

ALONSO ROMERO, Mª Paz, «El fuero universitario, siglos XIII-XIX», in *Historia de la Universidad de Salamanca. II. Estructuras y flujos*, Salamanca, Ediciones Universidad de Salamanca, 2004, pp. 161-188.

ÁLVAREZ VILLAR, Julián, *La Universidad de Salamanca. III. Arte y tradiciones*, Salamanca, Ediciones Universidad de Salamanca, 1990.

Amasuno Sarraga, Marcelino V., *La Escuela de Medicina del Estudio salmantino (siglos XIII-XV)*, Salamanca, Ediciones Universidad de Salamanca, 1990.

Beaujouan, Guy, *Manuscrits scientifiques médiévaux de l'Université de Salamanque et de ses «Colegios Mayores»*, Bordeaux, Féret et Fils, 1962.

Belloso Martín, Nuria, *Política y Humanismo en el siglo XV. El maestro Alfonso de Madrigal, el Tostado*, Valladolid, Universidad de Valladolid, 1989.

Beltrán de Heredia, Vicente, Los orígenes de la Universidad de Salamanca, Salamanca, Universidad de Salamanca, 1953.

Beltrán de Heredia, Vicente, *Bulario de la Universidad de Salamanca (1219-1549)*, I, Salamanca, Universidad de Salamanca, 1966.

Beltrán de Heredia, Vicente, *Bulario de la Universidad de Salamanca (1219-1549)*, II, Salamanca, Universidad de Salamanca, 1966.

Beltrán de Heredia, Vicente, *Bulario de la Universidad de Salamanca (1219-1549)*, III, Salamanca, Universidad de Salamanca, 1967.

Beltrán de Heredia, Vicente, *Cartulario de la Universidad de Salamanca, 1218-1600*, I, Salamanca, Universidad de Salamanca, 1970.

Beltrán de Heredia, Vicente, *Cartulario de la Universidad de Salamanca. La Universidad del Siglo de Oro*, II, Salamanca, Universidad de Salamanca, 1970.

Beltrán de Heredia, Vicente, «El convento de San Esteban en sus relaciones con la Iglesia y la Universidad de Salamanca durante los siglos XIII, XIV y XV», in *Miscelánea Beltrán de Heredia*, I, Salamanca, Editorial OPE, 1971, pp. 165-186.

Burgueño Arjono, Susana, *El saber astrológico a finales del siglo XV en la Universidad de Salamanca*, Salamanca, Ediciones Universidad de Salamanca, 2009. Collection Víctor of Doctoral theses, with CD.

Cantera Burgos, Francisco, *Abraham Zacut. Siglo XV*, Madrid, Aguilar, 1934.

Carabias Torres, Ana Mª, «Colegios Mayores y letrados, 1406-1516», in *La primera Escuela de Salamanca (1406-1516)*, Salamanca, Ediciones Universidad de Salamanca, 2012, pp. 15-34.

Castillo Vegas, José Luis, *Política y clases medias. El siglo XV y el maestro salmantino Fernando de Roa*, Valladolid, Universidad de Valladolid, 1987.

Castro y Castro, Manuel, *San Francisco de Salamanca y su Studium Generale*, Santiago de Compostela, Aldecoa, 1998.

Castro de Santamaría, Ana, *Juan de Álava, arquitecto del Renacimiento*, Salamanca, Caja Duero, 2001.

Chabás, José & Goldstein, Bernard R., *Abrahan Zacut (1452-1515) y la Astronomía en la Península Ibérica*, Salamanca, Ediciones Universidad de Salamanca, 2009.

Chacón, Pedro, *Historia de la Universidad de Salamanca*, ed. Ana Mª Carabias Torres, Salamanca, Ediciones Universidad de Salamanca, 1990.

Codoñer Merino, Carmen & González Iglesias, Juan Antonio, *Antonio de Nebrija: Edad Media y Renacimiento*, Salamanca, Ediciones Universidad de Salamanca, 1994.

Cortés Vázquez, Luis, *Ad Summum Caeli. El programa alegórico humanista de la escalera de la Universidad de Salamanca*, Salamanca, Ediciones Universidad de Salamanca, 1986.

De Dios de Dios, Salustiano, *El Consejo Real de Castilla (1385-1522)*, Madrid, Centro de Estudios Constitucionales, 1982.

De Dios de Dios, Salustiano & Torijano, Eugenia (coords.), *Cultura, política y práctica del Derecho. Juristas de Salamanca. Siglos XV-XX*, Salamanca, Ediciones Universidad de Salamanca, 2012.

De Dios de Dios, Salustiano, «Los juristas de Salamanca en el siglo xv», in *Cultura, política y práctica del Derecho. Juristas de Salamanca. Siglos XV-XX*, Salamanca, Ediciones Universidad de Salamanca, 2012, pp. 13-70.

Delgado, Buenaventura, *El Colegio de San Bartolomé de Salamanca. Privilegios, bienes, pleitos, deudas y catálogo biográfico de colegiales*, Salamanca, Ediciones Universidad de Salamanca, 1986.

Delgado Jara, Inmaculada & Herrera García, Rosa Mª, «Humanidades y humanistas en la Universidad de Salamanca del siglo xv», in *Salamanca y su Universidad en el primer Renacimiento: siglo XV. Miscelánea Alfonso IX*, 2010, Salamanca, Ediciones Universidad de Salamanca, 2011, pp. 241-265.

Delgado Jara, Inmaculada, «El Tostado y la exégesis bíblica», in *La primera Escuela de Salamanca (1406-1516)*, Salamanca, Ediciones Universidad de Salamanca, 2012, pp. 55-74.

Di Camillo, Ottavio, *El Humanismo castellano del siglo* XV, Valencia, Fernando Torres, 1976.

Esperabé Arteaga, Enrique, *Historia pragmática e interna de la Universidad de Salamanca. I. La Universidad de Salamanca y los Reyes*, Salamanca, Francisco Núñez Izquierdo, 1914.

Esperabé Arteaga, Enrique, *Historia pragmática e interna de la Universidad de Salamanca. II. Maestros y alumnos más distinguidos*, Salamanca, Francisco Núñez Izquierdo, 1917.

Espinel Marcos, José Luis & Hernández Martín, Ramón, *Colón en Salamanca: los dominicos*, Salamanca, Caja de Ahorros y Monte de Piedad, 1988.

Esteban, León, *Cultura y prehumanismo en la Curia pontificia del papa Luna (1394-1423)*, Valencia, Universidad de Valencia, 2002.

Febrero Lorenzo, Mª Asunción, «Un viejo colegio salmantino: el de Pan y Carbón», *Revista Calasancia*, VI, 22 (Madrid, 1960), pp. 233-248.

Fernández Álvarez, Manuel, «La reforma universitaria [de 1512]», *Stvdia Historica. Historia Moderna*, II, 3 (Salamanca, 1984), pp. 21-46.

Fernández Álvarez, Manuel (dir.), *La Universidad de Salamanca. Trayectoria histórica y proyecciones*, I, Salamanca, Ediciones Universidad de Salamanca, 1989.

Fernández Álvarez, Manuel (dir.), *La Universidad de Salamanca. II. Atmósfera intelectual y perspectivas de investigación*, Salamanca, Ediciones Universidad de Salamanca, 1990.

Fernández Gallardo, Luis, *Alonso de Cartagena (1385-1456). Una biografía política en la Castilla del siglo* XV, Valladolid, Junta de Castilla y León, 2002.

Fernández Vallina, Emiliano, «La importancia de Alfonso de Madrigal, el Tostado, Maestrescuela en la Universidad de Salamanca», in *Salamanca y su Universidad en el primer Renacimiento: siglo* XV. *Miscelánea Alfonso IX*, 2010, Salamanca, Ediciones Universidad de Salamanca, 2011, pp. 161-178.

FLÓREZ MIGUEL, Cirilo; GARCÍA CASTILLO, Pablo & ALBARES, Roberto, *El Humanismo científico*, Salamanca, Caja de Ahorros Provincial, 1988; reedición ampliada, 1999.

FLÓREZ MIGUEL, Cirilo, *La ciencia del cielo. Astrología y Filosofía natural en la Universidad de Salamanca (1450-1530)*, Salamanca, Caja de Ahorros y Monte de Piedad, 1989.

FLÓREZ MIGUEL, Cirilo, «Las ciencias y la Universidad de Salamanca en el siglo XV», in *Salamanca y su Universidad en el primer Renacimiento: siglo XV. Miscelánea Alfonso IX*, 2010, Salamanca, Ediciones Universidad de Salamanca, 2011, pp. 179-201.

FLÓREZ MIGUEL, Cirilo; HERNÁNDEZ, Maximiliano & ALBARES, Roberto (eds.), *La primera Escuela de Salamanca (1406-1516)*, Salamanca, Ediciones Universidad de Salamanca, 2012.

FUERTES HERREROS, José Luis, *Estatutos de la Universidad de Salamanca, 1529; mandato de Pérez de Oliva, rector*, Salamanca, Ediciones Universidad de Salamanca, 1984.

FUERTES HERREROS, José Luis, «Lógica y Filosofía, siglos XIII-XVII», in *Historia de la Universidad de Salamanca. III-1. Saberes y confluencias*, Salamanca, Ediciones Universidad de Salamanca, 2006, pp. 491-586.

FUERTES HERREROS, José Luis, «Pensamiento y Filosofía en la Universidad de Salamanca del siglo XV», in *Salamanca y su Universidad en el primer Renacimiento: siglo XV. Miscelánea Alfonso IX*, 2010, Salamanca, Ediciones Universidad de Salamanca, 2011, pp. 203-240.

GABAUDAN, Paulette, *El mito imperial. Estudio iconológico de los relieves de la Universidad salmantina*, Madrid, Éride Ediciones, 2012.

GALLEGO DE MIGUEL, Amelia, *Los doctores de la Reina y su casa en Salamanca*, Salamanca, Centro de Estudios Salmantinos, 1972.

GARCÍA BALLESTER, Luis, «El papel de las instituciones de consumo y difusión de la ciencia médica en la Castilla del siglo XIII; el monasterio, la catedral y la Universidad», *Dynamis*, 4 (1984), pp. 33-63.

GARCÍA BALLESTER, Luis, «Galenismo y enseñanza médica en la Universidad de Salamanca del siglo XV», *Dynamis*, 20 (Granada, 2000), pp. 209-247.

García Ballester, Luis (dir.), *Historia de la ciencia y de la técnica en la Corona de Castilla. I. Edad Media*, Valladolid, Junta de Castilla y León, 2002.

García Casar, Mª Fuencisla, *El pasado judío de Salamanca*, Salamanca, Diputación de Salamanca, 1987.

García de la Concha, Víctor (dir.), *Nebrija y la introducción del Renacimiento en España*, Salamanca, Universidad de Salamanca, 1981.

García Cruzado, Servando, *Gonzalo García de Villadiego, canonista salmantino del siglo xv*, Roma/Madrid, CSIC, 1968.

García Fraile, Dámaso, «La cátedra de Música de la Universidad de Salamanca durante diecisiete años del siglo xv (1464-1481)», *Anuario Musical*, 46 (Barcelona, 1991), pp. 57-101.

García y García, Antonio, «Los difíciles inicios (siglos xiii-xiv)», in *La Universidad de Salamanca. Trayectoria histórica y proyecciones*, I, Salamanca, Ediciones Universidad de Salamanca, 1989, pp. 13-34.

García y García, Antonio, «Consolidaciones del siglo xv», in *La Universidad de Salamanca. Trayectoria histórica y proyecciones*, I, Salamanca, Ediciones Universidad de Salamanca, 1989, pp. 35-58.

García y García, Antonio, «Nuevos descubrimientos sobre la canonística salmantina de los siglos xiv-xv», *Anuario de Historia del Derecho Español*, 50 (Madrid, 1980), pp. 361-374.

García y García, Antonio, «Manuscritos de Derecho canónico medieval en Salamanca», *Stvdia Gratiana*, 27 (Roma, 1996), pp. 105-148.

García y García, Antonio, «Juristas salmantinos, siglos xiv-xv. Manuscritos e impresos», in *Historia de la Universidad de Salamanca. III-1. Saberes y confluencias*, Salamanca, Ediciones Universidad de Salamanca, 2006, pp. 121-137.

García Zarza, Eugenio (coord.), «Salamanca y Colón». Monographic article in *Salamanca. Revista de Estudios*, 54 (Salamanca, 2006).

Gilli, Patrick; Verger, Jacques & Le Blévec, Daniel, *Les universités et la ville au Moyen Âge*, Leiden-Boston, Brill, 2007.

Gómez González, Pedro J. & Vicente Baz, Raúl, *Guía del Archivo y Biblioteca de la catedral de Salamanca*, Salamanca, Cabildo Catedral, 2007.

Gómez Redondo, Fernando, *Historia de la prosa de los Reyes Católicos, umbral del Renacimiento*, Madrid, Cátedra, 2012, 2 vols.

González, Julio, *El maestro Juan de Segovia y su biblioteca*, Madrid, CSIC, 1944.

González de la Calle, Pedro Urbano & Huarte y Echenique, Amalio, *Constituciones de la Universidad de Salamanca (1422). Edición paleográfica con prólogo y notas*, Madrid, Tipografía de la Revista de Archivos, Bibliotecas y Museos, 1927.

González de la Calle, Pedro Urbano, & Huarte y Echenique, Amalio, *Constituciones y bulas complementarias dadas a la Universidad de Salamanca por el pontífice Benedicto XIII, Pedro de Luna, edición paleográfica con prólogo y notas*, Zaragoza, 1932.

Goñi y Gaztambide, José, «Tres rótulos de la Universidad de Salamanca de 1391, 1389 y 1393», *Anthologica Annua*, 11 (Roma, 1963), pp. 227-336.

Goñi y Gaztambide, José, *Los españoles en el Concilio de Constanza. Notas biográficas*, Madrid/Barcelona, CSIC, 1966.

Gould y Quincy, Alicia, «Lucio Marineo Siculo (1444?-1536)», *Simancas. Estudios de Historia Moderna*, 1 (Valladolid, 1950), pp. 257-270.

Guadalupe Beraza, Mª Luisa; Martín Martín, José Luis; Vaca Lorenzo, Ángel & Villar García, L. M., *Colección documental del Archivo de la catedral de Salamanca (1098-1300)*, León, Centro de Estudios San Isidoro, 2010.

Guijarro González, Susana, «La formación cultural del clero catedralicio en la Salamanca medieval (siglos XII al XV)», in *Actas I Congreso de Historia de Salamanca, I*, Salamanca, Diputación de Salamanca, 1992, pp. 449-460.

Guijarro González, Susana, *Maestros, escuelas y libros. El universo cultural de las catedrales en la Castilla medieval*, Madrid, Universidad Carlos III & Editorial Dykinson, 2004.

Hernández Jiménez, Margarita, «Fuentes documentales del Archivo de la catedral de Salamanca relacionadas con su Universidad (1306-1556)», *Miscelánea Alfonso IX, 2002*, Salamanca, Ediciones Universidad de Salamanca, 2003, pp. 195-232.

Hernández Martín, Ramón, «El convento y Estudio de San Esteban», in *Historia de la Universidad de Salamanca. I. Trayectoria y vinculaciones*, Salamanca, Ediciones Universidad de Salamanca, 2002, pp. 589-612.

Hernández Montes, Benigno, *Biblioteca de Juan de Segovia. Edición y comentario de su escritura de donación*, Madrid, CSIC, 1984.

Jaramillo Guerreira, Miguel Ángel, «Documentación medieval en el Archivo universitario salmantino», in *Salamanca y su Universidad en el primer Renacimiento: siglo XV. Miscelánea Alfonso IX*, 2010, Salamanca, Ediciones Universidad de Salamanca, 2011, pp. 319-342.

Jiménez Calvete, Teresa, *Un siciliano en la España de los Reyes Católicos: las «Epistolum familiarium libri XVII» de Lucio Marineo Sículo*, Alcalá, Universidad de Alcalá, 2001.

Labajos Alonso, José, «Pedro de Osma, impulsor del Humanismo y del conocimiento de Aristóteles en Salamanca», *Cuadernos Salmantinos de Filosofía*, 22 (Salamanca, 1995), pp. 135-158.

Labajos Alonso, José, *Proceso contra Pedro de Osma*, Salamanca, Universidad Pontificia de Salamanca, 2010.

Labajos Alonso, José, «Pedro de Osma y Fernando de Roa: significación histórica», in *La primera Escuela de Salamanca (1406-1516)*, Salamanca, Ediciones Universidad de Salamanca, 2012, pp. 143-162.

Lahoz Gutiérrez, Lucía, «La imagen de la Universidad de Salamanca en el Cuatrocientos», in *Salamanca y su Universidad en el primer Renacimiento: siglo XV. Miscelánea Alfonso IX, 2010*, Salamanca, Ediciones Universidad de Salamanca, 2011, pp. 267-317.

Lahoz Gutiérrez, Lucía, «Primera imagen universitaria salmantina. Entre la vindicación pontificia y la poética mudéjar», in *Imagen, contextos morfológicos y universidades. Miscelánea Alfonso IX, 2012*, Salamanca, Ediciones Universidad de Salamanca, 2013, pp. 69-119.

López Alsina, Fernando; Oiza Galán, L. Jaime & Suárez Rodríguez, María de la O (coords.), *Alfonso IX e a súa época. Pro utilitate Regni mei*, Ayuntamiento de A Coruña & Ministerio de Cultura, A Coruña, 2008.

López Benito, Clara Isabel, *Bandos nobiliarios en Salamanca al iniciarse la Edad Moderna*, Salamanca, Centro de Estudios Salmantinos, 1983.

López de Goicoechea Zabala, Javier, *Dualismo cristiano y Estado moderno. Estudio histórico-crítico de la «Summa de Ecclesia» (1453) de Juan de Torquemada*, Salamanca, Universidad Pontificia, 2005.

Madrigal Terrazas, Santiago, *El pensamiento eclesial de Juan de Segovia (1393-1458). La gracia en el tiempo*, Madrid, Universidad Pontificia de Comillas, 2004.

Marcos Rodríguez, Florencio, «Los manuscritos de Alfonso de Madrigal conservados en la Biblioteca universitaria de Salamanca», *Salmanticensis*, 4 (Salamanca, 1957), pp. 3-50.

Marcos Rodríguez, Florencio, «La antigua biblioteca de la catedral de Salamanca», *Revista Hispania Sacra*, 14 (Madrid, 1961), pp. 281-319.

Marcos Rodríguez, Florencio, *Catálogo de documentos del Archivo catedralicio de Salamanca (siglos XII-XV)*, Salamanca, Universidad Pontificia de Salamanca, 1962.

Marcos Rodríguez, Florencio, *Extractos de los Libros de Claustros de la Universidad de Salamanca. Siglo XV (1464-1481)*, Salamanca, Universidad de Salamanca, 1964.

Marcos Rodríguez, Florencio, «Un cisma de rectores de la Universidad de Salamanca a fines del siglo XV», *Salmanticensis*, 14 (Salamanca, 1967), pp. 341-369.

Marcos Rodríguez, Florencio, «La Capilla de Santa Catalina de la catedral vieja y la historia de la Universidad de Salamanca», *Salmanticensis*, XXXI (Salamanca, 1984), pp. 225-244.

Marineo Sículo, Lucio, *De Hispaniae laudibus*, Burgos, 1497.

Martín Lamouroux, Fernando, *La revelación contable en la Salamanca histórica. La Universidad de Salamanca en la encrucijada contable de los siglos XV y XVI a través de sus cuentas*, Salamanca, Diputación de Salamanca, 1988.

Martín Lamouroux, Fernando, «Bases económicas. Hacienda universitaria, siglos XV y XVI», in *La Universidad de Salamanca. II. Atmósfera intelectual y perspectivas de investigación*, Salamanca, Ediciones Universidad de Salamanca, 1990, pp. 399-419.

Martín Martín, José Luis, *El cabildo de la catedral de Salamanca (siglos XII-XIII)*, Salamanca, Centro de Estudios Salmantinos, 1975.

Martín Martín, José Luis, «Estructura demográfica y profesional de Salamanca a finales de la Edad Media», *Salamanca. Revista de Estudios*, 1 (Salamanca, 1982), pp. 15-33.

Martín Martín, José Luis, *El patrimonio de la catedral de Salamanca. Un estudio de la ciudad y el campo salmantino en la Baja Edad Media*, Salamanca, Diputación de Salamanca, 1985.

Martín Martín, José Luis, «El Archivo de la catedral y la Historia de la Universidad de Salamanca», in *Historia de la Universidad de Salamanca. IV. Vestigios y entramados*, Salamanca, Ediciones Universidad de Salamanca, 2009, pp. 19-50.

Martín Martín, José Luis, «Universidad y catedral en el Cuatrocientos salmantino», in *Salamanca y su Universidad en el primer Renacimiento: siglo XV. Miscelánea Alfonso IX*, 2010, Salamanca, Ediciones Universidad de Salamanca, 2011, pp. 93-119.

Martín Martín, José Luis, «La Universidad para un Reino en expansión», in *La Universidad de Salamanca en el siglo XIII. Constituit Scholas fieri Salamanticae*, Salamanca, Ediciones Universidad de Salamanca, 2011, pp. 13-23.

Martín Rodríguez, José Luis, «Saber es poder. El Estudio salmantino», in *Historia de Salamanca. II. Edad Media*, Salamanca, Centro de Estudios Salmantinos, 1997, pp. 479-503.

Martínez Casado, Ángel, *Lope de Barrientos: un intelectual en la Corte de Juan II*, Salamanca, Editorial San Esteban, 1994.

Martínez Frías, José María, *El cielo de Salamanca. La bóveda de la antigua Biblioteca universitaria*, Salamanca, Ediciones Universidad de Salamanca, 2006.

Martínez Frías, José María, «La Real Capilla de San Jerónimo», in *Loci et imagines, imágenes y lugares, 800 años de patrimonio de la Universidad de Salamanca*, Salamanca, Ediciones Universidad de Salamanca, 2013, pp. 67-101.

Martínez de Osma, Pedro, *Comentario a la Ética de Aristóteles*. Critical edition by José Labajos Alonso, Salamanca, Universidad Pontificia, 1996.

Mínguez, José Mª (coord.), *Historia de Salamanca. II. Edad Media*, Salamanca, Centro de Estudios Salmantinos, 1997.

Monsalvo Antón, José Mª, «El Estudio y la ciudad en el período medieval», in *Historia de la Universidad de Salamanca*, I, Salamanca, Ediciones Universidad de Salamanca, 2002, pp. 435-465.

Monsalvo Antón, José Mª, «Poder y cultura en la Castilla de Juan II», in *Salamanca y su Universidad en el primer Renacimiento: siglo XV. Miscelánea Alfonso IX*, 2010, Salamanca, Ediciones Universidad de Salamanca, 2011, pp. 15-91.

Nieto Soria, Manuel, «La conflictividad en torno al diezmo en los comienzos de la crisis bajomedieval castellana, 1250-1315», *Anuario de Estudios Medievales*, 14 (Barcelona, 1984), pp. 211-235.

Nieto Soria, Manuel, *Iglesia y génesis del Estado Moderno en Castilla (1369-1480)*, Madrid, Universidad Complutense, 1993.

Nogaledo Álvarez, Santiago, *El Colegio Menor de Pan y Carbón, primero de los colegios universitarios de Salamanca (1386-1780)*, Salamanca, Universidad de Salamanca, 1958.

Olmedo, Félix G., *Nebrija en Salamanca (1475-1513)*, Madrid, Editora Nacional, 1944.

Orella y Unzué, José Luis de, *Partidos políticos en el primer Renacimiento (1340-1450)*, Madrid, Fundación Universitaria Española, 1976.

Payo Hernanz, René Jesús & De Berriochoa Sánchez Moreno, Valentín (coords.), *La catedral de Salamanca. Nueve siglos de historia y arte*, Salamanca, Promecal, 2012.

Pena González, Miguel Anxo, «Proyecto salmantino de Universidad pontificia e integración de la Teología en el siglo XV», in *Salamanca y su Universidad en el primer Renacimiento: siglo XV. Miscelánea Alfonso IX*, 2010, Salamanca, Ediciones Universidad de Salamanca, 2011, pp. 121-160.

Pereda, Felipe, *La arquitectura elocuente. El edificio de la Universidad de Salamanca bajo el reinado de Carlos V*, Madrid, Sociedad Estatal Centenarios, 2000.

Peset, Mariano & Gutiérrez Cuadrado, Juan, «Clérigos y juristas en la Baja Edad Media castellano-leonesa», *Senara*, 3 (Vigo, 1981), Anexo I, pp. 7-110.

Peset, Mariano, «La corporación en sus primeros siglos, xiii-xv», in *Historia de la Universidad de Salamanca. II. Estructuras y flujos*, Salamanca, Ediciones Universidad de Salamanca, 2004, pp. 19-35.

Peset, Mariano & García Trobat, Pilar, «Poderes y modelos universitarios, siglos xv-xix», in *Historia de la Universidad de Salamanca. II. Estructuras y flujos*, Salamanca, Ediciones Universidad de Salamanca, 2004, pp. 37-91.

Reinhardt, Klaus, *Pedro de Osma y su Comentario al símbolo «Quicumque»*, Madrid, Joyas bibliográficas, 1977.

Rico, Francisco, *Nebrija frente a los bárbaros*, Salamanca, Universidad de Salamanca, 1978.

Rodríguez G. de Ceballos, Alfonso, *Las catedrales de Salamanca*, León, Everest, 1978.

Rodríguez-San Pedro Bezares, Luis E. (coord.), *Historia de la Universidad de Salamanca. I. Trayectoria y vinculaciones*, Salamanca, Ediciones Universidad de Salamanca, 2002.

Rodríguez-San Pedro Bezares, Luis E. (coord.), *Historia de la Universidad de Salamanca. II. Estructuras y flujos*, Salamanca, Ediciones Universidad de Salamanca, 2004.

Rodríguez-San Pedro Bezares, Luis E. (coord.), *Historia de la Universidad de Salamanca.III-1 y III-2. Saberes y confluencias*, Salamanca, Ediciones Universidad de Salamanca, 2006, 2 vols.

Rodríguez-San Pedro Bezares, Luis E. & Polo Rodríguez, Juan Luis (coords.), *Historia de la Universidad de Salamanca. IV. Vestigios y entramados*, Salamanca, Ediciones Universidad de Salamanca, 2009.

Rodríguez-San Pedro Bezares, Luis E., «Diego de Anaya y Maldonado (1357-1437)», in *Diccionario Biográfico Español*, IV, Madrid, Real Academia de la Historia, 2010, pp. 183-190.

Rodríguez-San Pedro Bezares, Luis E. & Polo Rodríguez, Juan Luis (eds.), *Salamanca y su Universidad en el primer Renacimiento: siglo xv. Miscelánea Alfonso IX*, 2010, Salamanca, Ediciones Universidad de Salamanca, 2011.

Rummel, Erika, «Marineo Siculo: a protagonist of Humanism in Spain», *Renaissance Quaterly*, 50 (3) (New York, 1977), pp. 701-722.

Rupérez Almajano, Nieves, *El Colegio Mayor de San Bartolomé o de Anaya*, Salamanca, Ediciones Universidad de Salamanca, 2003.

Russo, Daniel, *Saint Jêrome en Italia, étude d'iconographie et de spiritualité, XIIIᵉ-XIVᵉ siècles*, Paris, 1987.

Sala Balust, Luis, *Catálogo de fuentes para la historia de los antiguos colegios seculares de Salamanca*, Madrid-Barcelona, Instituto Enrique Flórez, 1954.

Sala Balust, Luis, *Constituciones, estatutos y ceremonias de los antiguos colegios seculares de la Universidad de Salamanca*, III, Salamanca, Universidad de Salamanca, 1964.

Sánchez Caro, José Manuel; Herrera, Rosa Mª & Delgado, Mª Inmaculada, *Alfonso de Madrigal, el Tostado. Introducción al Evangelio según san Mateo*, Salamanca, Universidad Pontificia, 2008.

Sánchez y Sánchez, Daniel, «Catedral y Universidad en sus orígenes», in *La Universidad de Salamanca. I. Trayectoria histórica y proyecciones*, Salamanca, Universidad de Salamanca, 1989, pp. 323-338.

Sánchez y Sánchez, Daniel, *La catedral vieja de Salamanca*, Salamanca, Cabildo Catedral, 1991.

Sanz y Díaz, José, *Alonso de Madrigal*, Madrid, Publicaciones Españolas, 1957.

Sebastián, Santiago, «Un programa astrológico en la España del siglo xv», *Traza y Baza. Cuadernos Hispánicos de Simbología, Arte y Literatura*, 1 (Barcelona, 1972), pp. 49-61.

Veríssimo Serrão, Joaquim, *Portugueses no Estudo de Salamanca (1250-1550)*, Coimbra, Imprenta de Coimbra, 1962.

Soetermeer, Frank D., «Un professeur de l'Université de Salamanque au xiiiᵉ siècle, Guillaume d'Accurse», *Anuario de Historia del Derecho Español*, 54 (Madrid, 1985), pp. 753-765.

Suárez Fernández, Luis, *Benedicto XIII*, Barcelona, Ariel, 2002.

Vaca Lorenzo, Ángel, «Origen y formación del primitivo campus de la Universidad de Salamanca. Las Escuelas Mayores», *Salamanca. Revista de Estudios*, 43 (Salamanca, 1999), pp. 143-169.

Vaca Lorenzo, Ángel, «Le campus de l'Université de Salamanque au Moyen Âge. Besoins fonctionnels et réponses inmobilières», in *Les universités et la ville au Moyen Âge*, Leiden-Boston, Brill, 2007.

Valero García, Pilar, «Un aspecto del rectorado de Fernán Pérez de Oliva, pretendidos Estatutos de la Universidad de Salamanca bajo su mandato», *Stvdia Historica. Historia Moderna*, IV, 3 (Salamanca, 1986), pp. 51-74.

Valero García, Pilar & Pérez Martín, Manuel, «Pedro de Luna y el Estudio salmantino. Aspecto institucional: su Constitución», *Stvdia Historica. Historia Moderna*, VIII (Salamanca, 1990), pp. 131-149.

Valero García, Pilar & Pérez Martín, Manuel, *Constituciones de Martín V*. Edition, study and Spanish translation, Salamanca, Ediciones Universidad de Salamanca, 1991.

Vázquez Janeiro, Isaac, «El convento y Estudio de San Francisco», in *Historia de la Universidad de Salamanca. I. Trayectoria y vinculaciones*, Salamanca, Ediciones Universidad de Salamanca, 2002, pp. 613-633.

Vázquez Janeiro, Isaac, «La Teología en el siglo xv», in *Historia de la Universidad de Salamanca. III-1. Saberes y confluencias*, Salamanca, Ediciones Universidad de Salamanca, 2006, pp. 171-201.

Vicente Baz, Raúl, *Los libros de Actas capitulares de la catedral de Salamanca (1298-1489)*, Salamanca, Archivo Catedral, 2009.

Vindel, Francisco, *El arte tipográfico en España durante el siglo XV: Salamanca, Coria y Reino de Galicia*, Madrid, Dirección General de Relaciones Culturales, 1946.

Viñayo González, Antonio, «El colegio asturiano de Pan y Carbón, primer colegio secular universitario de Salamanca», *Boletín del Instituto de Estudios Asturianos*, VII, 20 (Oviedo, 1953), pp. 500-522.

Villarroel González, Óscar, *El Rey y el Papa. Política y diplomacia en los albores del Renacimiento (el siglo XV en Castilla)*, Madrid, Sílex, 2009.

Vv. Aa., *La Universidad de Salamanca en el siglo XIII. Constituit Scholas fieri Salamanticae*, Salamanca, Ediciones Universidad de Salamanca, 2011.

NOTES

[1]   «Hic salutari consilio evocavit magistros peritissimos in Sacris Scripturis, et constituit Scholas fieri Salamanticae»: *Chronicon mundi*. Cited by Vicente Beltrán de Heredia, *Cartulario de la Universidad de Salamanca, 1218-1600*, I, Salamanca, Universidad de Salamanca, 1970, p. 596. Lucas de Tuy refers to King Alfonso IX of León, and his narration takes place sometime after 1236. He refers to masters of Holy Scriptures, but he does not mention those of Law. On the other hand, the so-called founding document has not survived, if it ever existed at all. Towards 1570, according to the manuscript on the History of the University by master Chacón, the Archives did not have any document from the King Alfonso IX, and the information is conveyed «from what is said in a privilege granted by the King Ferdinand the Saint»: *Historia de la Universidad de Salamanca hecha por el maestro Pedro Chacón* (edited by Ana M.ª Carabias), Salamanca, Ediciones Universidad de Salamanca, 1990, p. 51. Chacón was positive about the King Alfonso IX exerting an unlimited protection: «But this King of León was not as rich as his cousin, the King of Castile, and he did not support [the Schools] nor did he appoint salaries for the masters who taught their lessons. He only defended and sheltered the lecturers and students who wanted to come here»: *op. cit.*, p. 52. However, at the end of the 13th century, the Franciscan friar Juan Gil de Zamora praised Alfonso IX as the founder of the University for being its patron and providing it with funds: «Apud Salamanticam Generale Studium de reditibus propriis ordinavit»: *Liber illustrium personarum sive Historiae canonicae et civilis*, Biblioteca Nacional de Madrid, ms. 2763, fol. 72v; cited by Beltrán de Heredia, *Cartulario*, I, *op. cit.*, pp. 623-624; the text is dated after 1282. Alfonso IX was staying in Salamanca, leading his troops, in October 1218, and from there he went to Cáceres, which was being held by the Muslims. He came back to Salamanca before heading towards Ciudad Rodrigo in February 1219; *Cf.* José Luis Martín Martín, «La Universidad para un Reino en expansión», in VV. AA., *La Universidad de Salamanca en el siglo XIII. Constituit Scholas fieri Salamanticae*, Salamanca, Ediciones Universidad de Salamanca, 2011, p. 13. The same autor, José Luis Martín Martín, points out in his research some circumstances regarding the connections between the King Alfonso IX and Salamanca: He had a wet nurse from Salamanca, María Ibáñez, and he was also in love with a lady from Salamanca, doña Maura, with whom he fathered an illegitimate son, Fernando Alfonso, Canon of the Cathedral since 1223 and later Archdeacon of Salamanca. This Fernando Alfonso may have been part of the first group of graduated students from Salamanca: «La Universidad para un Reino en expansión», *op. cit.*, pp. 14-15.

[2]   The Cathedral chapter of Salamanca was part of the institutional and cultural sphere of the Archbishopric of Santiago de Compostela. *Cf.* José Luis Martín Martín, *El cabildo de la catedral de Salamanca (siglos XII-XIII)*, Salamanca, Centro de Estudios Salmantinos, 1975, p. 46.

[3] Beltrán de Heredia points out that for the Studium of Salamanca, Alfonso IX had the assistance of the Cathedral clergy, who were well trained and had roots in Santiago de Compostela; *Cartulario*, I, *op. cit.*, pp. 43-53.

[4] José M.ª Monsalvo Antón, «El Estudio y la ciudad en el período medieval» in *Historia de la Universidad de Salamanca*, I, Salamanca, Ediciones Universidad de Salamanca, Salamanca, 2002, p. 437.

[5] Beltrán de Heredia, *Cartulario*, I, pp. 589-592. The Council of Lateran established that metropolitan Cathedrals would employ «a reader and a confessor in order to facilitate the implementation of the canons related to the study of the Holy Scriptures, preaching and annual confession». That is, the Cathedrals established the presence of a theologian or master of the Holy Scriptures: Vicente Beltrán de Heredia, *Bulario de la Universidad de Salamanca (1219-1549)*, I, Salamanca, Universidad de Salamanca, 1966, p. 181.

[6] There are references to 17 people with the title of *masters* in Salamanca in the 12th century, some of them of French and English origin: Susana Guijarro González, «La formación cultural del clero catedralicio en la Salamanca medieval (siglos XII al XV)», in *Actas del I Congreso de Historia de Salamanca*, I, Salamanca, Diputación de Salamanca, 1992, p. 451.

[7] According to José Luis Martín Martín «the Cathedral School kept on with its activities, apart from the University, during the entire Middle Ages. It developed a parallel teaching work, but on a different level, because it was in charge of the elementary training, which focused on the introduction to reading, writing, singing and basic notions of Latin», in «Universidad y catedral en el Cuatrocientos salmantino», *Salamanca y su Universidad en el primer Renacimiento: siglo XV. Miscelánea Alfonso IX*, 2011, Salamanca, Ediciones Universidad de Salamanca, 2012, pp. 103-104.

[8] This is the first document that has been kept in the University Archive of Salamanca (AUSA). The Salamanca corporation of the 13th century has left few documentary remains, and none of them are from the meetings in which the appointment of students and masters was decided. What we can deduce is based on royal and pontifical documents who answered to the demands of privileges and support from the academic guild. *Cf. La Universidad de Salamanca en el siglo XIII*, *op. cit.*, which includes pictures of the documents and their transcripts. It has been suggested that maybe there never was a founding charter of the Studium Generale strictly speaking: «The lack of such document may be explained just as with other corporations which began to operate merely with the support of an already existing organization which had some specific needs. In this case, the Cathedral chapter wanted to educate its community, and to do so it had a Cathedral School. The first signs of the incipient University would appear there, and they would later grow and become consolidated with the support of Kings and Popes». *Cf.* Miguel Ángel Jaramillo Guerreira, «Documentación medieval en el Archivo universitario salmantino», *Salamanca y su Universidad en el primer Renacimiento: siglo XV. Miscelánea Alfonso IX*, 2010, Salamanca, Ediciones Universidad de Salamanca, 2011, p. 325. The 60 first documents of the University Archive of Salamanca, up to the year 1414, are royal and pontifical documents, with the exception of a book of income and tithes from 1403: *ibidem*, p. 334.

[9] The objective was to protect the scholars from Salamanca and to establish an arbitral tribunal to solve conflicts. It was an echo of the «Habita» constitution granted by the Emperor Frederick I Barbarossa to protect the students of Bologna. *Cf.* M.ª Paz Alonso Romero, «Las Constituciones

medievales», in Luis E. Rodríguez-San Pedro (coord.), *Historia de la Universidad de Salamanca*, II, Salamanca, Ediciones Universidad de Salamanca, 2004, p. 95. The whole tribunal was established by Ferdinand III and it was made up of the Bishop of Salamanca, the Dean of the Cathedral chapter, the Prior of the Dominicans, the Custos of the Franciscans, five respectable men from Salamanca, one Canon from León and one Canon from Lamego. We can infer the importance of the clergy in these University beginnings and their origin from the environments of the Kingdom of León and Portugal.

[10] There is little information on this period. There is a testament dated in 1240 from the master Pedro, precentor of the Cathedral of Salamanca, in which some books of Law are mentioned: *Decretum, Digestum Vetus, Digestum Novum, Codex, Infortiatum,* Azo's *Summa, Libellus Institutionum. Cf.* Bernardo Alonso Rodríguez, «Las Escuelas de Cánones del Estudio salmantino en la Edad Media», in *Actas del Primer Congreso de Historia de Salamanca*, I, Salamanca, Diputación de Salamanca, 1992, p. 464. It seems that he was a person devoted to the study of Law. Since 1245, the Bishop and the Cathedral chapter of Salamanca are granted «the faculty to choose the most suitable people for the Studium during a period of five years, during which time, every incumbent of the Cathedral is exempted from compulsory residence»: Susana Guijarro González, «La formación cultural del clero catedralicio en la Salamanca medieval (siglos XII al XV)», in *Actas del Primer Congreso de Historia de Salamanca, op. cit.*, p. 454.

[11] Alfonso Rodríguez G. de Ceballos, *Las catedrales de Salamanca*, León, Everest, 1978, pp. 8-37. René Jesús Payo Hernanz & Valentín de Berriochoa Sánchez-Moreno (coords.), *La catedral de Salamanca. Nueve siglos de historia y arte*, Salamanca, Promeal, 2012.

[12] It is worth mentioning that the original document of this so-called «Magna Carta» by Alfonso X has not been preserved. The University Archive of Salamanca only has a copy that was transcribed and re-enveloped by Henry III in Valladolid on September 20th 1401.

[13] «The Kings founded, protected and funded an ecclesiastical center of studies made up of clergymen and subject to the ecclesiastical authorities»: M.ª Paz Alonso Romero, *Universidad y sociedad corporativa. Historia del privilegio jurisdiccional del Estudio salmantino*, Madrid, Tecnos, 1997, p. 15.

[14] The salaries assigned to the Chairs by Alfonso X in 1254 were probably deducted, as in the case of the University of Palencia, from part of the so-called Tercias Reales of the tithe (the third part of the Tercias de Fábrica). These Tercias Reales had been granted by the Pope to the King Ferdinand III so that he could finance his wars against the Muslims. Pedro Chacón, in his *Historia de la Universidad*, from around 1570, reveals that Alfonso X the Wise was the first king who provided Salamanca with income and salaries: «This funding was the first one that the University of Salamanca had had»: *Historia de la Universidad de Salamanca hecha por el maestro Pedro Chacón, op. cit.*, p. 60.

[15] A master of Law, with a salary of 500 maravedís per year, and a graduate with a temporary Chair. A master of Decrees, with 300 maravedís. Two masters of Decretals, with 500 maravedís. Two masters of Logic (Summulae and Dialectics), with 200 maravedís. Two masters of Grammar (Latin, Rhetoric, Poetics), with 200 maravedís. Two masters of Physics (Medicine), with 200 maravedís. One master of Organ (Music), with 50 maravedís. Also, there was funding for a library clerk who was in charge of copying the *pecias* or pieces of texts from the books, with 100 maravedís; and an apothecary or pharmacist, with 50 maravedís. Therefore, there were 3

Chairs of Canon law, 2 of Civil law, 2 of Medicine, 2 of Logic, 2 of Grammar and 1 of Music. The entire funding may be valued at approximately 2,500 maravedís: Beltrán de Heredia, *Bulario*, I, *op.cit.*, p. 46.

[16] «The constitutional and government model of the medieval Church and State were largely created by jurists, especially in the 12th and 13th centuries», based on the Roman law and the Canon law that were taught in the University of Bologna and the Roman Curia. *Cf.* Antonio García y García, «Los difíciles inicios (siglos XIII-XIV)», in Manuel Fernández Álvarez (dir.), *La Universidad de Salamanca. Trayectoria histórica y proyecciones*, I, Salamanca, Universidad de Salamanca, 1989, p. 29.

[17] In his *Partidas* (II Partida, 31) Alfonso X strongly defended the men from the academia and their usefulness for Kings: «...all men and nations and Kingdoms take advantage of wise men and they are cautious about them, and they follow their guidance». He mainly refers to jurists or experts in Law, to whom he grants an unusually high status: 1) Thay are seen as some sort of nobility, as «Lords of the Laws»; 2) Judges had to rise when they saw a Master of Laws; 3) These experts had direct access to the King or the Emperor; 4) After 20 years of teaching they were granted the title of «Counts». This was an intentional idealization that had no real reflection on the Universities of Castile in the 13th century. Also, the *Partidas* were not a binding legal text until the year 1347.

[18] By supporting the University corporation, the Pope also asserts its authority over Bishops and Kings.

[19] «The granting of a seal to a community or *universitas* entailed the recognition of a legal status to act». *Cf.* M.ª Paz Alonso Romero, «Las Constituciones medievales», *op. cit.*, p. 97.

[20] Since the pontifical bull of Alexander IV in 1255, «the *Maestrescuela* or master of the school became, by pontifical appointment, the only judge of the scholars of Salamanca, and this activity was no longer shared with the Bishop»: *Cf.* M.ª Paz Alonso Romero, «El fuero universitario, siglos XIII-XIX», in *Historia de la Universidad de Salamanca*, II, Salamanca, Ediciones Universidad de Salamanca, 2004, p. 163. «The value of the degrees that had been granted by royal decision was limited to the Kingdom itself. However, those that were granted by pontifical decision were recognized in the entire Christendom»: *Cf.* Beltrán de Heredia, *Bulario*, I, pp. 44-45.

[21] Antonio García y García, «Los difíciles inicios (siglos XIII-XIV)», *op. cit.*, p. 15.

[22] Frank D. Soetermeer, «Un professeur de l'Université de Salamanque au XIIIe siècle, Guillaume d'Accurse», in *Anuario de Historia del Derecho Español*, 54 (Madrid, 1985), pp. 753-765.

[23] Beltrán de Heredia already pointed out the influence of Bologna over Salamanca in the 13th and 14th centuries: *Cartulario*, I, p. 194. However, compared with the Bolognese model, the Kings gain more importance as patrons in Salamanca from the beginning.

[24] For Mariano Peset, «professors and doctors were part of the university meeting, unlike in Bologna, although the decisions were adopted by a majority of students and graduates»: Mariano Peset & Pilar García Trobat, «Poderes y modelos universitarios, siglos XV-XIX», in *Historia de la Universidad de Salamanca*, II, Salamanca, Ediciones Universidad de Salamanca, 2002, p. 39. In the *Partidas* of Alfonso X there were already references to the Rector: «Distinguished above all, he who is called in Latin Rector of the Studium»: *Partidas*, 2, 31, 6. In an open letter from Alfonso X dated on January 31st 1271 in Cuenca, there are references to «the masters of the University of Scholars of Salamanca»; and in another letter by Alfonso

X from Alcalá on January 1st 1276 there is a reference to «the University of the masters and the students of the Studium»: Enrique Esperabé Arteaga, *Historia pragmática e interna de la Universidad de Salamanca. I. La Universidad de Salamanca y los Reyes*, Salamanca, Francisco Núñez Izquierdo, 1914, pp. 24-25.

[25] «The deepest cause for the intense relations between the Cathedral chapter and the University are their members and the fact that, for many centuries, Canons were present at the University in all its spheres: ecclesiastical dignitaries, Canons and Prebendaries were, in different times and according to their personal circumstances, students, masters or university authorities»: José Luis Martín Martín, «El Archivo de la catedral y la historia de la Universidad de Salamanca», in Luis E. Rodríguez-San Pedro & Juan Luis Polo Rodríguez (coords.), *Historia de la Universidad de Salamanca. Vestigios y entramados*, IV, Salamanca, Ediciones Universidad de Salamanca, 2009, pp. 19-20.

[26] The lack of books of Medicine in the inventories of the Cathedral, and specifically in the book inventory of 1275, leads Luis García Ballester to put into question the effective teaching of Medicine in Salamanca during the 13th century. In any case, we know very little about the teaching of this discipline: «El papel de las instituciones de consumo y difusión de la ciencia médica en la Castilla del siglo XIII; el monasterio, la catedral y la Universidad», *Dynamis*, 4 (Granada, 1984), pp. 33-63.

[27] There are no references to a University library on those dates, but there are references of a library in the Cathedral, enriched by the contribution of the Bishop Domingo Martínez in 1267. Towards 1275, the inventories of the library of the Cathedral register about 60 books. Thirty of them were kept in two chests and they seem to be books of worship, missals, psalters, books of rites, gospels... Out of the remaining thirty, many of them are related to the Holy Scriptures, and there are also works by the Fathers of the Church. We can also find sermons, a book on theological questions and a book of Sentences. There were no books of Law, and there is only a succinct reference to some classics: Virgil's *Bucolics* and a book by Sallustius. On the other hand, it is unlikely that the members of the Cathedral chapter had any prominent libraries in the 13th century: some books, mainly of Law, especially *Decretals* and some works by Justinian, *Digestum vetus, Digestum novum, Codex...* Cf. José Luis Martín Martín, *El cabildo de la catedral de Salamanca...*, *op. cit.*, pp. 45-46. The Archdeacon of Salamanca, Alfonso Pérez, left, in his will from 1264, his library to the Cathedral chapter of Mondoñedo. The library was made up of the *Decretals, Digestum vetus, Codex, Digestum novum, Glossa* and other legal works. Cf. José Luis Martín Martín, «El Archivo de la catedral y la historia de la Universidad de Salamanca», *op. cit.*, p. 30. There are other wills from members of the Cathedral chapter of Salamanca from the second half of the 13th century that make reference to several books of Law they owned: *Decretum, Decretals, Digestum vetus, Digestum novum, Codex, Instituta, Infortiatum,* Azo's *Summa,* Accursius' *Glossa...* Cf. Bernardo Alonso Rodríguez, «Las Escuelas de Cánones del Estudio salmantino en la Edad Media», *op. cit.*, p. 466.

[28] Sancho IV ordered the lessors of the Tercias of the diocese to assist the University with the Royal Fifth of the dioceses of Armuña and Peña del Rey with a total amount of 11,600 maravedís: Beltrán de Heredia, *Cartulario*, I, p. 56.

[29] The third volume of the legal collections that make up the *Corpus iuris canonici.*

³⁰ Beltrán de Heredia, *Cartulario*, I, p. 103.

³¹ Ramón Hernández Martín, «El convento y Estudio de San Esteban», in Luis E. Rodríguez-San Pedro (coord.), *Historia de la Universidad de Salamanca*, I, Salamanca, Ediciones Universidad de Salamanca, 2002, p. 589. The first reference to the relation between the Dominicans and the University is a will from 1240: Master Pedro, cantor of the Cathedral and probably a professor of Law in the University, left the *Decretum* to Master Tiburcio, the glossed *Psalterium* to the Monastery of Sahagún, and the *Digestum novum* and other legal treatises to the Dominican Monastery of San Juan el Blanco. *Cf.* Vicente Beltrán de Heredia, «El convento de San Esteban en sus relaciones con la Iglesia y la Universidad de Salamanca durante los siglos XIII, XIV y XV», in *Miscelánea Beltrán de Heredia*, I, Salamanca, Editorial OPE, 1972, p. 169.

³² Isaac Vázquez Janeiro, «El convento y Estudio de San Francisco», in *Historia de la Universidad de Salamanca*, I, Salamanca, Ediciones Universidad de Salamanca, 2002, pp. 614, 615, 617. Manuel de Castro y Castro, *San Francisco de Salamanca y su Studium Generale*, Santiago de Compostela, Aldecoa, 1998.

³³ Mariano Peset, «La corporación en sus primeros siglos, XIII-XV», *Historia de la Universidad de Salamanca*, II, Salamanca, Ediciones Universidad de Salamanca, 2004, p. 29.

³⁴ Royal decree of Ferdinand IV, Ayllón, August 7ᵗʰ 1300: Esperabé, I, pp. 31-32. The King ordered «that the money from these Tercias is kept in a chest, that the chest is kept with the Treasury of the Cathedral and that three keys are distributed, one for the Dean of Salamanca on behalf of the Bishop and the Cathedral chapter, one for the Rectors who have the keys of the seal of the University and one for the custodians on behalf of the town council. And the custodians will distribute the income from the Tercias according to what has been ordered by the Bishop and to the usual custom with salaries and the payment of other officials of the Studium. All the necessary expenses for the Studium and the University will be paid for the maintenance of the Studium». The custodians had to provide an annual report of the money distribution to the Dean of the Cathedral chapter, the Rectors of the University and two good men from the town council. The board of accounts was scheduled for the 1ˢᵗ of July «in the church of the See», and a written record had to be kept.

³⁵ In the abovementioned royal decree from Ayllón, August 7ᵗʰ 1300, it states that: «Sometimes the masters stop their lectures due to the decrease in the payment of their salaries», p. 32.

³⁶ The tithe for the church was divided into Tercias or thirds, as is stated in the *Partidas*. One of them is for the Bishop, another for the clergy and another one for the maintenance of the churches. One third of this last Tercia de Fábrica (one ninth of the total tithe) was usually granted by the Popes to the medieval Kings for the funding of the war costs against the infidels. These grants had a limited validity, although the tithe was still collected as a custom, with the subsequent protests and suits between the Popes and the Kings. Therefore, the 2,500 maravedís granted by Alfonso X to the University of Salamanca for the funding of its Chairs in the 13ᵗʰ century came from the third part of the Tercia de Fábrica. And, when at the beginning of the 14ᵗʰ century, the Popes (Boniface VIII and Clement V) proved reluctant to extend the distribution of the Tercias to the University, the institution found itself unable to pay its masters. José Manuel Nieto Soria, «La conflictividad en torno al diezmo en los comienzos de la crisis

bajomedieval castellana, 1250-1315», *Anuario de Estudios Medievales*, 14 (Barcelona, 1984), pp. 211-235.

[37] Beltrán de Heredia, *Bulario*, I, pp. 327, 330: Bull of Anagni, September 16th 1301 and bull of Grausello, October 14th 1313. Beltrán de Heredia, *Cartulario*, I, p. 116. The University Archive does not contain documentation on its patrimony during the first two centuries (13th and 14th), because the institution did not possess many lands or properties, only the Tercias from the tithe, and they were not administered directly, but by means of a renting system: Miguel Ángel Jaramillo Guerreira, «Documentación medieval en el Archivo universitario salmantino», *op. cit.*, p. 336.

[38] «This University, up to the beginning of the 15th century or the end of the 14th century, was almost exclusively a Studium for jurists, canonists and legists which coexisted with other preparatory schools, such as the School of Grammar»: Salustiano de Dios de Dios, «Los juristas de Salamanca en el siglo XV», in Salustiano de Dios & Eugenia Torijano (coords.), *Cultura, política y práctica del Derecho. Juristas de Salamanca. Siglos XV-XX*, Salamanca, Ediciones Universidad de Salamanca, 2012, p. 20. The date of October 14th 1313 is significant because it is the moment when Clement V ordered the Archbishop of Santiago to pay the salaries of the professors of Salamanca: «In Decretis, Decretalibus, Legibus, Medicina, Logicalibus et Grammaticalibus et Musica», *Bulario*, I, pp. 330-331, which takes us closer to the actual teaching programs.

[39] Marcelino V. Amasuno Sarraga questions «the potential teaching and learning activity in the school of Medicine of the Studium of Salamanca» during the 13th century. In any case, it considers the situation as a «state of languor» that goes on during the 14th century: *La Escuela de Medicina del Estudio salmantino (siglos XIII-XV)*, Salamanca, Ediciones Universidad de Salamanca, 1990, pp. 29, 35. The first teacher of Medicine that has been documented was Lorenzo Juan, a graduate and lecturer in Salamanca which was mentioned in the Pontifical rotulus of expectative graces of August 1363 (Urban V). Marcelino V. Amasuno's assessment of the school of Medicine during the period prior to 1380 is that it went through «long years of mediocre survival»: *op. cit.*, p. 44.

[40] Antonio García y García, «Los difíciles inicios (siglos XIII-XIV)», *op. cit.*, p. 28.

[41] Bernardo Alonso Rodríguez, «Las Escuelas de Cánones del Estudio salmantino en la Edad Media», p. 467.

[42] Mariano Peset & Pilar García Trobat, «Poderes y modelos…», *op. cit.*, p. 39.

[43] «Everything suggests that, far from improving, as was the dream of Alfonso X the Wise, the School decayed due to the lack of support and of its own or external resources»: *Bulario*, I, p. 46. Masters and scholars «fled from Castile in pursuit of a more propitious environment for their studies»: *ibidem*, p. 48. Later on, Beltrán de Heredia summarizes the situation of Salamanca before the intervention of the Pope Benedict XIII: «A limited, mediocre and poorly paid teaching staff that indoctrinates a group of young people with an uncertain future; that is the essence of the first of our academies», *Bulario*, I, p. 83.

[44] Specifically, Avignon, June 9th 1363: *Bulario*, I, p. 53, 386-387. The same Urban V was responsible for a first failed attempt (June 1364) to establish a University school in Salamanca.

[45] Benefices for the academic staff from Castile; Avignon, September 17th 1365: *Bulario*, I, p. 401. Rotulus of a group of Spaniards, mainly

belonging to the scholar guild, who had to follow their studies in Avignon; Avignon, August 21ˢᵗ 1366: *Bulario*, I, pp. 403-408. One example of the granting of individual privileges is the awarding of a Canonry in Burgos to Alfonso Pérez, graduate *in utroque*, treasurer of Astorga and Canon of Toledo, by which he had to establish an accommodation for sixteen students in Salamanca; Avignon, February 20ᵗʰ 1364: *Bulario*, I, pp. 393-394. By request of the Chapter of Segovia, the position of Archdeacon of that church is granted to Gonzalo Núñez, who had been a graduate and a lecturer of Canons for four years in Salamanca; Avignon, April 25ᵗʰ 1364: *Bulario*, I, p. 396. Granting of a Canonry to Fernando Fernández, student of Canons in Rome, Avignon and Salamanca; Avignon, March 19ᵗʰ 1375: *Bulario*, I, p. 423.

[46] The University Archive has 318 documents dated from 1214 and 1500: 14 of them date from the 13ᵗʰ century, 15 from the 14ᵗʰ century and 289 from the 15ᵗʰ century. This bears witness to the relative importance of this medieval institution because «what has been kept is probably more related to the lack of other documents than with their loss». And the same author, at other point, states that: «the Archive keeps most of the medieval documents that it once had». *Cf.* Miguel Ángel Jaramillo Guerreira, «Documentación medieval en el Archivo universitario salmantino», *op. cit.*, pp. 333, 337.

[47] Daniel Sánchez y Sánchez, *La catedral vieja de Salamanca*, Salamanca, Cabildo catedral, 1991.

[48] In May 1381, in the Old Cathedral of Salamanca, the King of Castile entered the obedience to the Pope of Avignon, Clement VII, before the Cardinal Pedro de Luna, which would later become Benedict XIII. This is the beginning of an uninterrupted contact between the future Pope and the University of Salamanca. Pedro de Luna had studied Canons in Montpellier, he had a good legal training and he was a book lover. As a pontifical legate, he toured the European courts and achieved the political obedience of Castile (1381), Aragon (1387), Navarre (1390), France, Brabant, Scotland, England and Ireland (1393) for the Avignon Papacy, but he failed to obtain the obedience of Portugal. *Cf.* Luis Suárez Fernández, *Benedicto XIII*, Barcelona, Ariel, 2002.

[49] The future Benedict XIII would officially establish the Faculty of Theology in 1411, maybe with the precedent of the Constitutions of 1381. Prior to that point, these teachings were connected to the monasteries of the Dominicans and the Franciscans. Therefore, when the Vespers Chair of Theology of Salamanca was left vacant after the Franciscan Alfonso de Argüello was promoted, it was granted by means of a papal bull to the graduate Diego de Mayorga, from the same Order; Pont-de-Sorges, August 24ᵗʰ 1403: *Bulario*, I, p. 551. In 1405, the Dominican Martín de Sevilla received an authorization to be promoted to a teaching position in Theology after being a lecturer of Sentences in Salamanca; Genoa, July 17ᵗʰ 1405: *Bulario*, I, p. 595. In 1407, the Dominican Diego de Mayorga was promoted from the Vespers Chair of Theology of Salamanca to the position of Provincial Superior of Santiago, and the Chair was granted to Lope de San Ramón, a member of the same Order and graduate in Theology: Villafranca, September 18ᵗʰ 1407: *Bulario*, I, pp. 615-616. For some authors, the primitive alternation between Franciscans and Dominicans in the Chairs of Theology of the monasteries of Salamanca seems to be broken between 1407 and 1410, and some conflicts between both Orders become noticeable: Miguel Anxo Pena González, «Proyecto salmantino de Universidad pontificia e integración de la Teología en el siglo xv», in *Salamanca y su Universidad en el primer Renacimiento: siglo xv. Miscelánea Alfonso IX, 2010*, Salamanca, Ediciones Universidad de Salamanca, 2011, p. 138.

⁵⁰ General rotulus of expective graces granted by Clement VII to the academic staff of Salamanca; Avignon, May 29ᵗʰ-31ˢᵗ 1381: *Bulario*, I, pp. 57-58, 433-452. We present here some cases of personal privileges: A Canonry in Zamora is granted to Andrés Fernández, Decrees graduate by Avignon; Avignon, October 21ˢᵗ 1394: *Bulario*, I, p. 514. A Canonry in Ávila is granted to Jorge Domínguez, Laws graduate by Avignon; Avignon, October 21ˢᵗ 1394: *Bulario*, I, p. 515. A Canonry in Compostela is granted to Lope Fernández, Decrees graduate, regent of the Nones Chair in Salamanca and counselor of the University; Avignon, October 21ˢᵗ 1394: *Bulario*, I, p. 517. José Goñi Gaztambide, «Tres rótulos de la Universidad de Salamanca de 1391, 1389 y 1393», *Anthologica Annua*, 11 (Roma, 1963), pp. 227-336.

⁵¹ Raúl Vicente Baz, *Los libros de Actas capitulares de la catedral de Salamanca (1298-1489)*, Salamanca, Archivo de la Catedral, 2009, p. 152, No. 169 (November 22ⁿᵈ 1378); p. 200, No. 325 (April 11ᵗʰ 1404).

⁵² In October 1394, Benedict XIII was crowned Pope in Avignon, «Benedict XIII would maintain until 1417, the date of his deposition [in the Council of Constance], a clear policy of protection of the scholar guild. He would always give preference to the University of Salamanca in order to turn it into the first Academy of the Hispanic world, to the detriment of the University of Paris, which had turned its back on him […]. It can be rightfully said of him that he was the restorer and sort of a new founder of our University»: V. Beltrán de Heredia, *Bulario*, I, p. 72. For more information on the importance of the humanism or pre-humanism of Avignon in the origins of the Hispanic humanism: León Esteban, *Cultura y prehumanismo en la Curia pontificia del papa Luna (1394-1423)*, Valencia, Universidad, 2002.

⁵³ Little is known about the lost pontifical Constitutions of 1381. For Vicente Beltrán de Heredia, that is the moment when the single Rector and the voting system for professorships by the students was established: *Bulario*, I, p. 93; *Cartulario*, I, p. 197. The Cardinal Pedro de Luna had received orders from the Pope Clement VII to inspect and visit the Schools of Salamanca.

⁵⁴ Vicente Beltrán de Heredia, *Bulario de la Universidad de Salamanca (1219-1549)*, II, Salamanca, Universidad de Salamanca, 1966, pp. 24-37, dates these Constitutions in Peñíscola, according to a lost original text that had been transcribed by E. Denifle. Due to the French pressures, the Pope Benedict XIII left Avignon in March 1403. After a stay in Marseille and Genoa, he resided in Perpignan from the summer of 1408. There, he organized a Council in November, with the assistance of representatives from the University of Salamanca. In February 1411, he was in Calatayud, and he travelled around other territories of the Crown of Aragón. From December 1415, he shut himself away with his court in Peñíscola until 1423. *Cf.* Luis Suárez Fernández, *Benedicto XIII*, *op. cit.*, pp. 192, 200, 209, 241 & 293. Pedro Urbano González de la Calle & Amalio Huarte y Echenique, *Constituciones y bulas complementarias dadas a la Universidad de Salamanca por el pontífice Benedicto XIII, Pedro de Luna. Edición paleográfica, con prólogo y notas*, Zaragoza, 1932. Pilar Valero García & Manuel Pérez Martín, «Pedro de Luna y el Estudio salmantino. Aspecto institucional: su Constitución», *Studia Historica. Historia Moderna*, VIII (Salamanca, 1990), pp. 131-149: with a Spanish translation of the Constitutions of 1411.

⁵⁵ In 1407, Benedict XIII asked for prayers for the University of Salamanca and the success of his planned interview with the Pope Gregory XII. This is a sign of his close relation with the University of Salamanca; Marseille, January 31ˢᵗ 1407: *Bulario*, I, pp. 604-605.

[56] Apart from Salamanca, there were other Studia Generalia that benefited from the protection and support of Benedict XIII, such as Perpignan, Toulouse, Valladolid, Lérida and St. Andrews, in Scotland. *Cf.* Luis Suárez Fernández, *Benedicto XIII, op. cit.*, p. 304.

[57] The papacy of Avignon, during the Schism, was interested in favouring the ecclesiastics and University scholars who could have an influence on the Kings of Castile: *Bulario*, I, p. 62. The Rotuli of expectative graces succeeded each other. Rotulus of expectative graces of the master of the Order of Santiago for several students of Salamanca; Avignon, March 1st 1388: *Bulario*, I, p. 468. Rotulus of the University of Salamanca for part of its staff; Avignon, February 6th 1389: *Bulario*, I, p. 469. Rotulus of graces for scholars of Salamanca, presented by Juan Rodríguez, ambassador of the King of Castile; Avignon, February 18th 1389: *Bulario*, I, p. 472. Rotulus presented by Alfonso, Bishop of Zamora, which grants graces and benefices to students of Salamanca, Lérida and Avignon; Avignon, December 22nd 1391: *Bulario*, I, 482. Rotulus of expectative graces for thirty-six people from the University of Salamanca; Avignon, October 12th 1392: *Bulario*, I, pp. 490-493. Rotulus of expectative graces presented by the University of Salamanca for its own academic staff; Avignon, August 9th 1393: *Bulario*, I, pp. 496-505. Rotulus of expectatives for several students of Salamanca; Avignon, October 21st-27th 1394: *Bulario*, I, p. 535. Granting of expectative graces for several students of Salamanca; Avignon, October 29th-31st 1394: *Bulario*, I, p. 540. Expectative graces for four relatives of Toribio García de Sahagún, professor of the Prime Chair of Decrees in Salamanca and ambassador of the University to the Curia of Benedict XIII; Salon, October 14th 1403: *Bulario*, I, p. 556. Rotulus of expectative graces for the academic staff of Salamanca; Salon, October 16th-17th 1403: *Bulario*, I, pp. 560-562. General rotulus of Benedict XIII for the University of Salamanca; Salon, October 19th-23th 1403: *Bulario*, I, pp. 566-582; with interesting references to faculties and places of origin.

[58] «In the Constitutions of 1411, Benedict XIII included almost everything that he had presented in the Constitutions of 1381 when he was a visitor in the University, and at the end of the Constitutions of 1411 he added that the text from the old Constitutions of 1381 would remain valid: «In quantum praeventibus non contradicunt». He confirmed their effect «de apostolicae potestatis plenitudine» and cancelled whatever had been said to the contrary. According to this clause, some dispositions were into effect and appeared again in the Constitutions of 1422 without appearing in the Constitutions of 1411»: *Bulario*, I, pp. 73-74.

[59] Although it is probable that they already existed in the Constitutions of 1381. Someone called Gome Arias de Luiña was a counselor and student in Salamanca in the year 1391-1392. In the rotulus of expectative graces of 1381, created by the University, there are three counselors: Juan Alfonso de la Guardia, Gome Arias de Luiña and Fernando González de Grajal: *Bulario*, I, pp. 60, 61. Counselors are expressly mentioned in the Constitutions of 1411, but their number is not specified.

[60] This point can be inferred from a Royal Order from Juan II of Castile issued in Valladolid on February 14th 1411 in which he urges the town council, the inhabitants and the noblemen of Salamanca not to interfere in the matters of the Studium, which lead to disturbances, injuries and deaths. *Cf.* Enrique Esperabé Arteaga, *Historia pragmática e interna de la Universidad de Salamanca*, I, *op. cit.*, pp. 87-88. These orders were announced before the Rector elections, the votes for Chairs and other events.

[61] «The Maestrescuela was a member of the Cathedral chapter in charge of teaching Theology in the chapters of all the Latin Christendom and,

whenever they were available, he was also in charge of any other kinds of Schools of other levels in the chapter». *Cf.* Antonio García y García, «Consolidaciones del siglo xv», in Manuel Fernández Álvarez (dir.), *La Universidad de Salamanca. Trayectoria histórica y proyecciones*, I, Salamanca, Universidad de Salamanca, 1989, p. 38. Henry III of Castile, with a Royal order from Valladolid, August 20th 1391, accepted the Maestrescuela of the Cathedral as the exclusive judge of the University guild, with no other intervention of any lay or royal judge: Esperabé, I, *op. cit.*, p. 38.

[62] Bull of Peñíscola, July 26th 1411: *Bulario*, II, p. 38.

[63] Salustiano de Dios, «Los juristas de Salamanca en el siglo xv», *op. cit.*, p. 28.

[64] Royal order, Ayllón, November 4th 1411. The Kings conceived their relation with the University as a bond of special protection and tutelage. In a Royal Order of February 14th 1411, Juan II stated: «It is my duty to support it, because I am the patron of the Studium and it is greatly beneficial for my Kingdom». And in a Royal Order of November 1411 he added: «The Studium has a special status in my Kingdom, and I am its patron. It must be under my protection and my care, and I want to support it and defend it». *Cf.* Esperabé, I, pp. 87, 94. After certain hesitation, the Kings of Castile decided to support the authority of the Pope, because although conciliarism involved a certain autonomy of the Church in their kingdoms, its success would affect the very nature of their own power and their relation with the people through the Cortes (the political institution that represented the three Estates in medieval Spain): Salustiano de Dios, «Los juristas de Salamanca en el siglo xv», *op. cit.*, p. 36; Óscar Villarroel González, *El Rey y el Papa. Política y diplomacia en los albores del Renacimiento (el siglo xv en Castilla)*, Madrid, Sílex, 2009. In order to put the situation into context, we must take into account the fact that, during the reign of Juan II (1406-1453), Castile displayed an important diplomatic activity through its ambassadors and right-hand men, both jurists and men from the Church, mainly in relation with France, Burgundy and Italy, which also established a series of well-defined cultural channels: José M.ª Monsalvo Antón, «Poder y cultura en la Castilla de Juan II», in *Salamanca y su Universidad en el primer Renacimiento: siglo xv. Miscelánea Alfonso IX*, 2010, Salamanca, Ediciones Universidad de Salamanca, 2011, p. 33.

[65] «He regulated the allocation of salaries among the professors, he confirmed a second Tercia de Fábrica for the University and he began the construction of the Escuelas Mayores building. He promoted the residence for poor students, he established the Faculty of Theology after the defection of Paris, which supported the other Pope. He even founded the first College of San Bartolomé, which, together with others, would actively participate in the life and the struggles of the University. The King Juan II of Castile collaborated with great interest in these ventures: He granted again more authority to the council and the custodians so that they could punish any tumult or racket, he helped the Maestrescuela and the vice-chancellor (who actually was the second-in-command after the Maestrescuela); he turned the Jewish quarter of the Rúa Nueva into the residence for poor students, because most of the Jews had already converted; and he took the new Schools under his protection, because armed men used to gather at the doors in order to wound or kill students»: Mariano Peset, «La corporación en sus primeros siglos, xiii-xv», *op. cit.*, p. 34. For M.ª Paz Alonso Romero, the initiatives of the Pope Benedict XIII represented «a true re-foundation of the Centre», in «Las Constituciones medievales», *op. cit.*, p. 98. Vicente Beltrán de Heredia considers Benedict XIII as «the restorer and new founder of our University», *Bulario*, I, p.72.

[66] He ordered that all outstanding debts for the rent were collected and that the income was assigned to the construction of classrooms and a library and to the purchase of books; Peñíscola, September 13th 1413: *Bulario*, II, pp. 60-61: «Ipsius Studii in fabricandas certas domos pro auditoribus studentium et legentium in eodem, ac in nonnullos libros amendos et quamdam aliam domum pro hujusmodi libris tenendis integre converterentur».

[67] *Bulario*, I, p. 75 & *Bulario*, II, p. 82-83.

[68] He had already established Theology teachings in 1381 and 1411: *Cartulario*, I, pp. 225 onwards. Theology was taught in Salamanca in the monasteries of the Dominicans and Franciscans «at least since the beginning of the 14th century». Benedict XIII redesigned the Faculty of Theology with his bull *sincerae devotionis*, from March 16th 1416: Four chairs are created, two Prime chairs and two Vespers Chairs in the buildings of the University and another two in the monasteries of San Esteban and San Francisco. The courses and engagements of bachelors and graduates are also regulated. Towards 1419 a Chair of Bible studies is created in the University. *Cf. Bulario*, I, pp. 76, 80-81 & *Bulario*, II, pp. 79-82. We can see that, from Peñíscola, during the entire year 1416, Benedict XIII kept granting graces and benefits, and his Chancellery was still in full operation. The situation would change after he was deposed in July 1417 in the Council of Constance.

[69] Dispensation to García González de Quirós, an illegitimate son who studied Canons in Salamanca and Bologna, granting him access to certain benefits; Marseille, July 5th 1407: *Bulario*, I, pp. 610-611. Dispensation to Juan Martínez de Requena, graduate in Decrees by Avignon, letting him receive his doctorate in Salamanca or in Valladolid; Zaragoza, January 7th 1411: *Bulario*, II, p. 20. Authorization for Martín López de Hinestrosa, relative of Queen Catherine, to let him study abroad, even in Universities who did not pay obeisance to Benedict XIII; Peñíscola, September 27th 1411: *Bulario*, II, pp. 41-42. Commission to assign a vacant place to Juan Fernández de Villarreal in the Halls of Pan y Carbón of Salamanca; Peñíscola, February 5th 1417: *Bulario*, II, pp. 87-88.

[70] This is a chapter record of 1378. The beadle reports the necessary repairs for the building, such as wooden floors, seats against the walls and benches in the middle of the classrooms so that the students can have their books in front of them. The building had a capacity of 300 students. It all had to be done following the model of the Schools of Laws: Vicente Beltrán de Heredia, «La Universidad en el siglo xv», in *Cartulario de la Universidad de Salamanca. La Universidad en el Siglo de Oro*, II, Salamanca, Universidad de Salamanca, 1970, pp. 195-196. Ángel Vaca Lorenzo, «Origen y formación del primitivo campus de la Universidad de Salamanca. Las Escuelas Mayores», *Salamanca. Revista de Estudios*, 43 (Salamanca, 1999), p. 145.

[71] It was a space «with its teacher's chair and its benches»: Beltrán de Heredia, «La Universidad en el siglo xv», pp. 196-197.

[72] In the 3rd Constitution of 1411, the expenses of the University estate are regulated. First of all, the expenses of the 24 tenured Chairs had to be paid. The remainder would be used for the construction of seven classrooms, and after they had been built, the surplus from each year would be allocated to the purchase of books for the different Faculties: «Illud quod restabit cum aliis pecuniis arcae universitatis praedictae in fabricandas domos por quatuor auditoriis iuristarum et tribus theologorum, medicorum et philosophorum». This is the design of a whole constructive program which, due to the lack of resources, was delayed until 1415.

[73] Royal Order of Juan II of Castile, May 25th 1420: Esperabé, I, p. 99: «The University has built the Schools in which the Sciences are taught with a gallery and a courtyard in the middle in that same town». Lucía Lahoz, «Primera imagen universitaria salmantina. Entre la vindicación pontificia y la poética mudéjar», en *Imagen, contextos morfológicos y universidades. Miscelánea Alfonso IX, 2012*, Salamanca, Ediciones Universidad de Salamanca, 2013, pp. 69-119.

[74] A papal bull of September 13th 1413 granted indulgences to those who contributed to the support of the University: Beltrán de Heredia, *Bulario*, II, p. 61.

[75] Beltrán de Heredia, *Bulario*, I, pp. 74-75. Benedict XIII mentions the collections in the 2nd Constitution, and he stipulates that they had to be moderate. These collections still existed in 1460, and in 1480 it was agreed to abolish them.

[76] Beltrán de Heredia, «La Universidad en el siglo xv», *Cartulario*, II, p. 219. This is the economic breakdown of the different Chairs: Prime Chairs of Canons and Laws, 7,250 old maravedís each; Vespers Chairs of Canons and Laws, 3,100 old maravedís each; Prime Chair of Theology: 3,740 old maravedís; Vespers Chair of Theology, half of 3,740 if the holder is only a graduate; Prime Chair of Medicine, 2,200 old maravedís; Vespers Chair of Medicine, 1,400 old maravedís; Chairs of Grammar, Logic and Natural Philosophy, around 2,000 old maravedís each; the rest of the Chairs did not reach 1,000 old maravedís. The 7th Constitution of 1411 establishes the equivalence of the new gold florins or *«símiles»* and the old maravedís for the funding of the Chairs.

[77] Luis E. Rodríguez-San Pedro Bezares, «Diego de Anaya y Maldonado (1357-1437)», in *Diccionario biográfico español*, IV, Madrid, Real Academia de la Historia, 2009, pp. 184-185. Some authors have associated the emerging bureaucracy of the halls of residence and colleges with the service to the civil administration of the Kings, but this association would only appear later and it would become consolidated in the monarchy of the 16th and 17th centuries. In the 15th century, San Bartolomé consisted of two chaplains and fifteen residents, and these fifteen students received scholarships, five for theologians and ten for canonists. This exemplifies the predominance of sciences and ecclesiastical functions in this new University design. *Cf.* Ana M.ª Carabias Torres, «Colegios Mayores y letrados, 1406-1516», in Cirilo Flórez Miguel *et al.* (eds.), *La primera Escuela de Salamanca (1406-1516)*, Salamanca, Ediciones Universidad de Salamanca, 2012, pp. 15-34 and specifially p. 31. These fifteen scholarships, ten for canonists and five for theologians, are established in the Constitutions of 1414-1416: Luis Sala Balust, *Constituciones, estatutos y ceremonias de los antiguos colegios seculares de la Universidad de Salamanca*, III, Salamanca, Universidad de Salamanca, 1964, pp. 13, 14, 46. Diego de Anaya was himself a jurist. He had been trained in Salamanca in both laws.

[78] From Constance, Diego de Anaya returned to Spain via Lombardy, and he visited the College of San Clemente de los Españoles, founded in Bologna according to the testament of the Cardinal Gil de Albornoz in 1364. He also acquired different books and manuscripts. The College of San Clemente would act as the model which inspired him for the final touches of the College of San Bartolomé in Salamanca. Between 1417 and 1420, Anaya chose fifteen students and two chaplains from the kingdom of Castile, jurists and theologians, he dressed them with dun habits and a strip of cloth and a ribbon, and after a mass celebrated on the day of Saint John the Evangelist, they were established as a hall of residence with bulls

and privileges. Martin V confirmed their status in Constance with a bull on November 29th 1417. The College also had a set of Constitutions from around 1414-1416 adapted from those of the College of Bologna, which were reformed in 1435-1437: *Cf.* Rodríguez-San Pedro, «Diego de Anaya», *op. cit.*, p. 187. In appreciation of the results of the conclave in Constance, the now Pope Martin V promoted Diego de Anaya to the Archbishopric of Seville on March 16th 1410. However, in the following years, Diego de Anaya's enemies accused him of ambiguity and untruthfulness in his relation with Martin V, as well as of aligning himself with the deposed Benedict XIII: «Back in Spain, Anaya maintained his relation with the deposed Pontiff, and he did not even show the proper caution that was necessary for his own interest». *Cf. Bulario*, I, p. 109 and *Bulario*, II, pp. 92-94. Martín V had exempted the College of San Bartolomé from the jurisdiction of the Bishop, and he had added an extra two hundred annual florins from the diocese of Cuenca for the necessary repairs. Constance, December 14th 1417: *Bulario*, II, p. 95.

[79] That is the text of a Royal Order of May 25th 1420 on the armed conflicts in the Schools: «The University has built the Schools in which Sciences are taught with a gallery and a courtyard in the middle in that same town, and it is said that sometimes there are people who, with great temerity and nerve, and without fear of me or the justice, wait for the students who come to attend their lessons. And when these students enter the Schools and the courtyard, they and their relatives are attacked by these armed men. And these armed men start fights and quarrels with them and try to hurt them and kill them». Esperabé, *op. cit.*, I, p. 99.

[80] Royal Order, Aguilar de Campoo, May 16th 1421: Esperabé, *op. cit.*, I, pp. 104-106.

[81] «The students and their masters, as well as their families, enjoyed tax exemptions, they were not obliged to pay rent for their houses to the King or his officers, they did not participate in the rounds or patrols, and they were subject to special regulations with regard to house renting. Also, the town council had the authority to regulate wine trade, but students were not subject to the town regulations on the limitations imposed on wines from other places. The students complained to the King about the extra taxes imposed by the town council on the acquisition of food or other products, and the Studium refused to pay them, and it demanded to authorize said taxes before they could be imposed. Also, the Studium wanted to control its own livestock market and it refused to accept the town's controls on meat sales. All these elements were regarded by the city as a direct attack to their municipal sovereignty and dignity». *Cf.* José María Monsalvo Antón, «El Estudio y la ciudad en el período medieval», *op. cit.*, pp. 459-460.

[82] In 1419, by request of the last Rectors, Rodrigo Sánchez de Moscoso and Juan López de Illescas; together with a professor of Theology, Brother Juan de Santo Tomás; and two professors of Decrees, Martín de Galos and Alfonso de Villegas, who lived in the Holy See, the Pope entrusts the Archbishop of Santiago with the modification of the Constitutions of 1411 with the assistance of two suffragan Bishops and six members of the University. The University assembly named two doctors and four students to prepare the reform; bull of Ferrara, February 9th 1419: *Bulario*, II, pp. 125-126.

[83] Pedro Urbano González de la Calle & Amalio Huarte y Echenique, *Constituciones de la Universidad de Salamanca (1422). Edición paleográfica con prólogo y notas*, Madrid, Tipografía de la Revista de Archivos, Bibliotecas y Museos, 1927. *Constituciones de Martín V*. Edition and study by Pilar

Valero García and Manuel Pérez Martín, Salamanca, Ediciones Universidad de Salamanca, 1991: Latin facsimile and Spanish translation.

[84] The change in obeisance to the Pope would lead to ambiguity and trouble among the partisans of Benedict XIII. In 1422, Martin V himself ordered the suspension of Diego de Anaya, Archbishop of Seville, charged with leading a cryptic campaign against the Council of Constance. However, thanks to the intervention of the King Juan II of Castile, the Pope established that, if Anaya justified the accusations admitted the error of his ways, his position would be restored. Tivoli, September 13th 1422: *Bulario*, II, pp. 219-220.

[85] «Studium Salamantinum quod unum de quatuor orbis generalibus Studiis […] in regione Hispanica celebri fama resplendet»: Constitutions of 1422, 31, in Beltrán de Heredia, *Bulario*, II, p. 203.

[86] «The great families of Salamanca spread their tentacles into the most influential institutions and they put their most suitable members in charge of them». For this reason, the papal Constitutions of 1411 and 1422 prohibited the election of Rectors and counselors who came from the town of Salamanca or who had resided in it for a long time. *Cf.* José Luis Martín Martín, «Universidad y catedral en el Cuatrocientos Salmantino», in *Salamanca y su Universidad en el primer Renacimiento: siglo XV. Miscelánea Alfonso IX*, 2010, Salamanca, Ediciones Universidad de Salamanca, 2011, p. 118.

[87] The Rector, in turn, paid obeisance to the Church, the Pope and the observance of the Constitutions: Constitutions of 1422, 6th, 4th and 2nd.

[88] *Bulario*, I, p. 93.

[89] The Maestrescuela of the Cathedral was originally chosen by the Cathedral chapter, but since the 13th century, the appointment was decided in the pontifical Curia. Thanks to the pressures of the University, the Constitutions of 1422 assigned the election to the Senate. The Cathedral chapter of Salamanca complained and, in 1425, the appointment of the Maestrescuela was assigned back to them between 1426 and 1439. In this last date, the election went back to the Senate (with the authorization of the Holy See) thanks to a papal decision of Eugene IV: Florence, May 1st 1439: *Bulario*, II, p. 443. Plea of the Bishop and the Cathedral chapter of Salamanca to be restored the right to appoint the Maestrescuela; Rome, May 6th 1425: *Bulario*, II, p. 267. Martín V revoked the concession by which the University Senate of Salamanca could appoint the Maestrescuela and granted the right back to the Cathedral chapter; Rome, January 11th 1426: *Bulario*, II, pp. 278-279.

[90] M.ª Paz Alonso Romero, «El fuero universitario, siglos XIII-XIX», *op. cit.*, pp. 166, 174. The full authority of the Maestrescuela of Salamanca as an exclusive judge, chancellor, apostolic executor and custodian of the Studium is presented in the Constitutions of 1411 and 1422. The characteristics of his position seem to be influenced by the Parisian tradition, in which the jurisdiction of the Schools depended on the Bishop and the Chancellor. In many Studia Generalia, however, the jurisdiction depends on the Rector, as Mariano Peset pointed out in his works: Bologna, Lérida, Valladolid, Alcalá de Henares, Mexico, Lima… However, the jurisdictional model of the Maestrescuela of Salamanca was established in Lérida in 1585, in Cervera in 1717 and in the University of Caracas in 1740. However, in Lérida, from the 16th century, that jurisdiction was transferred to the Maestrescuela.

[91] «Juxta vota ipsorum studentium».

[92] *Bulario*, I, pp. 81-82.

93 Questions and requirements for graduation in the Constitutions of 1422, number 15, 16 and 17. The exams in the cathedral are established in the 18th Constitution. The exam had to be taken in a chapel of the Cathedral and it must last between one and two hours. The votes were registered in paper with the inscription «A» (for «approved», or *aprobado*) or «R» (for «failed», or *reprobado*).

94 *Bulario*, I, p. 98.

95 Martin V grants Juan II of Castile and his successors the Tercias de Fábrica for the war against the infidels, with some exemptions, such as those which are reserved for the University of Salamanca; Rome, October 8th 1421: *Bulario*, II, pp. 169-170. «Ever since Constance, the new Pope Martin V, whose pontificate would last from 1417 to 1431, would reward Juan II of Castile with Tercias and economic compensation, as well as those who supported him, and he would grant important privileges, as in the case of Diego de Anaya, for example»: José M.ª Monsalvo Antón, «Poder y cultura en la Castilla de Juan II», *op. cit.*, p. 34. In 1421, Juan II of Castile was rewarded 80,000 florins by means of a papal order of payment, thanks to the efforts of the King for his cause.

96 The Pope granted Juan Alfonso de Benavente, graduate in Decrees and in Arts, the Vespers Chair of Decrees which was vacant in Salamanca due to the reassignment of Alfonso de Reliegos; Rome, July 16th 1423: *Bulario*, II, pp. 239-240. Order for the abbot of Valladolid to grant the Vespers Chair of Canons in the new Schools («Scholarum novarum») of Salamanca to Pedro Gómez, graduate *in utroque*; Rome, October 30th 1423: *Bulario*, II, pp. 247-248.

97 Authorization for Juan González de Valdenebro, Chancellor of the Queen of Castile, to earn his doctorate in Decrees outside the Studium; Rome, January 11th 1425: *Bulario*, II, p. 263. Authorization for the Dominican friar Alfonso de Burgos, bachelor in Theology, to be promoted to a Magister's degree outside the Studium; Rome, March 25th 1426: *Bulario*, II, pp. 283-284. Authorization for Fernando González de Sepúlveda, bachelor in Decrees by the University of Salamanca, to earn his doctorate in a different Studium; Genzano, August 23rd 1426: *Bulario*, II, pp. 287-288. Pedro Sánchez de Segovia, bachelor in Decrees and resident in the Royal Curia of Castile, asks for permission to earn his doctorate outside the Studium; Rome, January 7th 1428: *Bulario*, II, p. 316. Permission to earn his doctorate outside the Studium for Fernando Muñoz, from Ciudad Real, bachelor in Laws, who had attended the Universities of Salamanca and Valladolid; Rome, June 25th 1428: *Bulario*, II, p. 321. Authorization for Juan Bernárdez, graduate in civil Law and bachelor in Decrees, student in Salamanca and Avignon, to earn his doctorate outside the Studium; Genzano, July 31st 1428: *Bulario*, II, p. 323. Authorization for Álvaro Martínez, Carmelite friar, who studied in Oxford, Salamanca and Lérida, to earn his Magisterium in Theology in the Studium of the Curia; Rome, February 15th 1429: *Bulario*, II, p. 329. These grants let us appreciate the academic itineraries of that period: Salamanca, Valladolid, Lérida, Avignon, the Studium of the Roman Curia...

98 Martin V grants a retirement to the professors of Salamanca after they had imparted lessons themselves for ten academic years; Rome, August 21st 1430: *Bulario*, II, pp. 340-341.

99 We can find bulls granting graces, privileges, benefits and posts (canonries, archdeaconries, archpriestries, deaneries...); compatibility of benefits, dispensations on illegitimacy, age or physical handicaps; leaves of absence for professors and masters; exemptions for a period of time, or for courses and lectures; dispensations to graduate outside the Studium (which

abounded in the decade of 1420): Beltrán de Heredia, *Bulario*, II, pp. 9 onwards.

[100] Rome, February 24th 1432: *Bulario*, II, pp. 354-356.

[101] The custodianships of the University of Salamanca were assigned to the Archbishop of Toledo, the Bishop of León and the scholastic representative from Salamanca: *Bulario*, II, pp. 356-358.

[102] Eugene IV gives the right to appoint the Maestrescuela of the Cathedral chapter and the Chancellor of the Studium back to the University Senate of Salamanca; Florence, May 1st 1439: *Bulario*, II, pp. 443-444.

[103] Assignment for the Bishop of Plasencia and Salamanca and for Juan Serrano, Prior of Guadalupe, to reform the Constitutions of the University of Salamanca; Rome, January 1st 1433: *Bulario*, II, p. 373.

[104] Cancellation of the Constitutions prepared by the University of Salamanca at the request of the late Archbishop of Santiago and restoration of the Constitutions confirmed by Martin V; Rome, November 10th 1446: *Bulario*, II, p. 541-542.

[105] In the Senate meeting with the Rector, the professors and the representatives on February 24th 1466, those present voiced their concerns over «whether Martin's Constitution revokes that of Benedict»: *Libros de Claustros* (AUSA), 1, fol. 67v. Florencio Marcos Rodríguez, *Extractos de los Libros de Claustros de la Universidad de Salamanca. Siglo XV (1464-1481)*, Salamanca, Universidad de Salamanca, 1964, p. 82.

[106] Also, «in the Roman Studium, since the time of Martin V, the studies and promotion to degrees in the Faculty of Law were facilitated, without the obstacles of the incompatibility with the possession of a curated benefice of Common law»: *Bulario*, I, p. 130.

[107] *Bulario*, I, p. 133.

[108] Beltrán de Heredia, *Cartulario*, I, p. 122. He did it with a Royal Decree in Tordesillas on May 2nd 1397 and a Royal Order in Tordesillas on May 8th 1397; *Cf*. Esperabé, I, pp. 45 onwards.

[109] *Bulario*, I, p. 75 and *Bulario*, II, pp. 82-83.

[110] Luis E. Rodríguez-San Pedro & Juan Luis Polo Rodríguez, «La Hacienda tradicional, siglos XV-XVIII», in *Historia de la Universidad de Salamanca*, II, Salamanca, Ediciones Universidad de Salamanca, 2004, p. 295.

[111] The minute books from the 15th century to which we have access let us locate the references to these main coffers of the Studium, because there were other chests with different functions. According to the meeting on July 10th 1465, the chest was located in the Library: «Pedro de León opened the Library where the chest was and they took out a box with gold». Along the 15th century, the chest was moved through several rooms: library, chapel, house of the beadle... Florencio Marcos Rodríguez, *Extractos de los Libros de Claustros, op. cit.*, p. 74.

[112] There are references on the participation of Jews from Salamanca and Alba de Tormes in the collection of the Tercias from the tithe for the University of Salamanca in the decades of 1430 and 1440: M.ª Fuencisla García Casar, *El pasado judío de Salamanca*, Salamanca, Diputación de Salamanca, 1987, pp. 133-134.

[113] Along the 15th century, the rent payments were made some days before Christmas, Easter and St. John's Day, in June.

[114] The University archive has few materials on the institutional economy of the period between 1218 and 1500. It is reduced to two books: *Libros de Rentas y Tercias*: 1403-1408 (AUSA. 1647) and 1435-1447 (AUSA. 1648).

[115] The total amount between 1403 and 1408 ranged between 156,000 and 196,000 annual maravedís. Between 1435 and 1439, it ranged between 236,000 and 343,000 maravedís. From 1440 to 1445 it ranged between 245,000 and 436,000 maravedís per year. *Cf.* Fernando Martín Lamouroux, *La revelación contable en la Salamanca histórica. La Universidad de Salamanca en la encrucijada contable de los siglos XV y XVI a través de sus cuentas,* Salamanca, Diputación de Salamanca, 1988, pages 160-161 provide a detailed account of the Tercias in the periods 1403-1408 and 1435-1447.

[116] Luis E. Rodríguez-San Pedro & Juan Luis Polo Rodríguez, «La Hacienda tradicional, siglos XV-XVIII», *op.cit.*, p. 302.

[117] Around 1569, the first historian of the University presented this interpretation of the situation: «[...] in the year 1411, the Pope Benedict XIII, who as we said, had visited, reformed and enlarged the Studium of Salamanca when he was a legate Cardinal in Spain with the fatherly love he felt for this University, after lengthy deliberations and advice created a set of Constitutions for its government. The rents from the Tercias had increased, so he added salaries to the Prime and Vespers Chairs of Theology and Medicine and to the Vespers Chair of Canons and to others who had been left poor the first time; and he created other Chairs anew. The number of salaries, which we will now refer to as tenured Chairs, reached twenty-five, as follows: Six of Canons, four of Laws, three of Theology, two of Medicine, two of Natural and Moral Philosophy, two of Logic, one of Astrology, one of Music, one of Hebrew, Chaldean and Arabic Languages, one of Rhetoric and two of Grammar. All these Chairs were assigned a certain amount of florins as a salary and they are being paid until now»: *Historia de la Universidad de Salamanca hecha por el maestro Chacón (1569),* edited by Ana M.ª Carabias Torres, Salamanca, Ediciones Universidad de Salamanca, 1990, p. 80.

[118] In a plea on February 24th 1432 addressed to the Pope Eugene IV, the tenured Chairs of the University are finally established as a total of twenty-five. Beltrán de Heredia, «La Universidad en el siglo XV», pp. 217.

[119] Bernardo Alonso Rodríguez, «En torno a los canonistas medievales salmantinos», *Proceedings of the Fifth International Congress of Medieval Canon Law, Salamanca, 1976,* Roma, Città del Vaticano, 1980, pp. 267-296.

[120] Beltrán de Heredia, «La Universidad del siglo XV», p. 218. The second Vespers Chair of Canons reappeared in an undetermined date, because both of them coexisted at the beginning of the 16th century.

[121] The Monastery of San Francisco of Salamanca was regarded as a Studium Generale of the Order towards the middle of the 14th century. There are references to graduates and students of Theology in this Studium Generale in the second half of the 14th century. Some of them had studied in other European universities such as Paris, Oxford, Cambridge, the Studium of the Roman Curia, Toulouse... *Cf.* Isaac Vázquez Janeiro, «El convento y Estudio de San Francisco», *op. cit.*, pp. 617-618.

[122] The studies at San Esteban were prominent. For some authors, in the Chair of Theology of San Esteban «the elite of the clergy of Salamanca was educated in that period», p. 594. In the second half of the 15th century there are also some Dominicans in the Prime and Vespers Chairs of Theology of the University.

[123] Constance, May 10th 1418: *Bulario,* II, pp. 107-108. In January 1419, Martin V increased the salary of the Chair of Bible studies by 100 florins: *Bulario,* II, p. 123, Mantua, January 21st 1419.

[124] Constitutions of 1422, 31st and 32nd Constitution. This made it possible «for the different Orders to establish in Salamanca their centers of theological education»: Miguel Anxo Pena González, «Proyecto salmantino

de Universidad pontificia...», *op. cit.*, p. 147. The same author deduces two different theological itineraries from the Constitutions of 1422: «A traditional one [...] for mendicants, mainly Franciscans and Dominicans, which had the University of Paris and the great Studia Generalia of the Orders in that city as a model; and a second one, which is not being emphasized in the Constitutions of Martin V, and which is mainly aimed at secular clergy and non-mendicant members of the religious orders», pp. 152-153.

[125] The Franciscan observants of the 15th century rejected the University degrees and turned their back to the possibility of holding Chairs. Fray Pedro de Villacreces set the precedent. He had studied in Toulouse and been a lecturer in the Monastery of San Francisco in Salamanca. In 1396 he got the degree of Master in Theology. Then, after a sudden conversion, he initiated an eremitic reformation in which he rejected the studies. The following statement is attributed to him: «I received in Salamanca the degree of Master, which I do not deserve; however, I learnt more inside my cell, crying in the darkness, than studying in Salamanca or Toulouse or Paris by the light of a candle». For strict observants, the degrees represented a decline of traditions. *Cf.* Vázquez Janeiro, «El convento y Estudio de San Francisco», pp. 618, 624. Pontifical bull of June 28th 1441 in which Brother Alonso de Canales is commanded to reform the Monastery of San Francisco of Salamanca. From this date, the Franciscans withdrew from the study and the academic teachings of the University and they fell back into their cloisters: *Bulario*, I, p. 143. Since 1453 there are also movements within the Dominican observants who asked for the incorporation of the monastery of San Esteban of Salamanca. Contrary to the Franciscans, a pontifical bull of March 15th 1479 would defend the traditions of Saint Stephen and their dedication to a regular life and to studies: *Bulario*, I, p. 144.

[126] Beltrán de Heredia, *Cartulario*, II, p. 219.

[127] *Ibidem*, p. 219.

[128] *Ibidem*, p. 219.

[129] These were the stages that the student had to go through when preparing his lessons, according to Benavente: «First of all, a general reading in order to reveal the meaning of the text and to retain what has been read; that is, a first attempt to understand and assimilate the text. In the second stage, the text has to be fragmented into units that allow an easier comprehension in order to demarcate and define the matter that is being studied and to finally create a summary of the text. In the third stage, the student will proceed to prepare a comprehensive explanation of the text, which requires the assistance of the glossators. The fourth reading extracts all the legal implications from the text for the formulation of the *notabilia*. Finally, in the fifth reading, the commentary is approached via the formulation of questions, opinions and solutions. The *notae mixtae* and the *notae supremae* are extracted from them, and they lead to the full comprehension of the legal text»: Luis Fernández Gallardo, *Alonso de Cartagena (1385-1456)*, Valladolid, Junta de Castilla y León, 2002, p. 77. He follows Juan Alfonso de Benavente, *Ars et doctrina studendi et docendi*. Critical edition by Bernardo Alonso Rodríguez, Salamanca, Universidad Pontificia de Salamanca, 1972, pp. 66-75. On the other hand, Benavente advises that the students use the vernacular when they deal with practical questions during the master classes (Law of the Kingdom?): Benavente, *op. cit.*, p. 97.

[130] Antonio García y García, «Consolidaciones del siglo xv», *op. cit.*, pp. 47.

[131] The 7th Constitution of 1422 allowed bachelors who wanted to become graduates to work as lecturers in the Schools or outside them.

[132] «You intend to and you do, de facto and against the law, meddle in the allocation of Chairs in the Studium when they are vacant. You give your support and help to some people, and try to get them those Chairs, either with threats or by force, or with pleas or intimidation or any other means necessary»: Royal Order, Ciudad Real, April 30th 1431; Esperabé, I, pp. 117-119.

[133] *Bulario*, II, pp. 177 onwards.

[134] Plea dated in Florence, April 22nd 1419, *Bulario*, II, pp. 128-130. It was granted in the bull «Sapientiae de cujus immarcescibile»; but it was not fully implemented due to the new Constitutions of 1422.

[135] Santiago Nogaledo Álvarez, *El Colegio Menor de Pan y Carbón, primero de los colegios universitarios de Salamanca (1386-1780)*, Salamanca, Universidad de Salamanca, 1958.

[136] The intellectual requirements for the benefices increased, although many privileges were granted through nepotism, political services, family influences and lineage. Some Bishops of Salamanca favored the dedication to study of the members of their dioceses. That is the case of Gonzalo de Vivero. In 1455, this Bishop met with his chapter and approved a statute that regulated the situation of the students with benefices, who would have the right to receive their rations and yearly shares even if they were in town but did not attend the offices. The Bishop thought that the intellectual education «highly ennobles those who have it, and so it gives great honor and benefits for the Church of God». *Cf.* José Luis Martín Martín, «El Archivo de la catedral y la historia de la Universidad de Salamanca», p. 36.

[137] «Until the 15th century we almost cannot find in Salamanca a single renowned canonist»: Antonio García y García, «Juristas salmantinos, siglos *XIV-XV*. Manuscritos e impresos», in Luis E. Rodríguez-San Pedro (coord.), *Historia de la Universidad de Salamanca. III-1. Saberes y confluencias*, Salamanca, Ediciones Universidad de Salamanca, 2006, p. 121. The Constitutions of 1411 of Benedict XIII order the purchase, among other books, of the works of «Petri Ioannis, doctoris Salamantini».

[138] «There are several motivations that explain the preponderance of the studies of ecclesiastical Law, such as the possibility of holding a position in the Church by graduates, without giving up their posts in the royal court, but also, and not less important, the fact that the possession of ecclesiastical benefices from an early age made it possible to carry on with expensive studies and to obtain degrees that would not have been received otherwise. However, there may also be other doctrinal reasons, such as the belief, commonly held by canonists, that Canon law was closer to Natural and Divine law than the study of Civil, Roman or Cesarean law»: Salustiano de Dios de Dios, «Los juristas de Salamanca en el siglo XV», in Salustiano de Dios & Eugenia Torijano (coords.), *Cultura, política y práctica del Derecho. Juristas de Salamanca, siglos XV-XX*, Salamanca, Ediciones Universidad de Salamanca, 2012, p. 17.

[139] Salustiano de Dios, «Los juristas de Salamanca en el siglo XV», *op. cit.*, p. 17, 43.

[140] «Jurists who came from Salamanca or who taught there [in the first two thirds of the 15th century] followed the path of the so-called «mos italicus», common among civilists and canonists, but with traditional methods. This did not mean that in their disputes and discussions they did not require other knowledge that the one found in the normative texts and in the works by the authorities on jurisprudence. They were also versed,

like their Italian models, in the study of the Bible, the Fathers of the
Church, classical history and Spanish history, and they also did not hesitate
to use texts by Aristotle, Cicero or Seneca, or even by theologians, if they
were required in their discussions. This was especially the case with some
particularly cultured jurists, such as Alonso de Cartagena, Rodrigo Sánchez
de Arévalo or even Juan Alfonso de Benavente and, of course, Alfonso
de Madrigal, El Tostado, who was more of a theologian than a jurist, and
who had therefore been educated in the Arts, which were not a previous
requirement for jurists, and not even for canonists»: Salustiano de Dios,
«Los juristas de Salamanca en el siglo xv», p. 48.

[141] «The most famous jurists until the reign of the Catholic Monarchs,
such as Arias de Balboa, Alfonso de Cartagena, Rodrigo Sánchez de Arévalo
or Juan Arias Dávila, not to mention the greatest Castilian jurist in the entire
15th century, Alfonso Díaz de Montalvo, were not related to the University
of Salamanca after becoming graduates or doctors»: Salustiano de Dios,
«Los juristas de Salamanca en el siglo xv», p. 18. On the presence of jurists
in the government and justice administration in Castile: José Manuel Nieto
Soria, *Iglesia y génesis del Estado Moderno en Castilla (1369-1480)*, Madrid,
Universidad Complutense, 1993.

[142] That is the opinion of Antonio García y García, «Consolidaciones
del siglo xv», *op. cit.*, pp. 52-53. Also Beltrán de Heredia, *Bulario*, I, pp.
120-121. Conciliarists «were in favor of the superiority of the Council over
the Pope, because it represented the universal Church, which had received
all its power from Christ, as had been stated in the «Fiequens» decree of
the Council of Constance and later developed in the Basel context with
the «Sacrosanta» decree. These texts were based on the ideas spread by the
theologians from Paris and used in that specific situation to end with the
papal schism in view of the failure of other possible solutions»: Salustiano de
Dios, «Los juristas de Salamanca en el siglo xv», p. 33. Others defended «the
supremacy of the Pope over the Council, because the Pontiff represented
the head of the Church and he had full authority, directly received from
Christ, so that the canons and decrees of the Council had no value without
the confirmation of the Pope, who had the authority over the creation,
dissolution and suspension of the Council»: *ibidem*, p. 35.

[143] Some authors maintain that there was a conciliarist breeding ground
in the early College of San Bartolomé: «It would not be very far-fetched to
think that the College of San Bartolome were originally a place where the
conciliarist theses were well received and supported»: Miguel Anxo Pena
González, «Proyecto salmantino de Universidad pontificia…», p. 134. The
author bases his opinion on the personality of Diego de Anaya, «a vehement
and belligerent man», and on his later confrontations with Martin V, and
also on the fact that «some of the most prominent and renowned scholars
also defended those theses; as in the case of Mella or El Tostado», p. 135.

[144] José Goñi Gaztambide, *Los españoles en el Concilio de Constanza.
Notas biográficas*, Madrid/Barcelona, CSIC, 1966. José Luis de Orella y
Unzué, *Partidos políticos en el primer Renacimiento (1340-1450)*, Madrid,
Fundación Universitaria Española, 1976. «Salamanca cannot be compared
with other small European universities, either new or not, which are at
the service of local provincial oligarchies. Instead, as a great global center
of knowledge in its first Golden Age, the 15th century, the University of
Salamanca showed a universalist and international spirit». *Cf.* José M.ª
Monsalvo Antón, «El Estudio y la ciudad en el período medieval», p. 456.
Castile sent approximately 130 participants to Basel.

[145] The Council of Basel was inaugurated in 1431; it was transferred to Ferrara in 1439; to Florence in 1439 and to Rome in 1443. When it moved to Ferrara, a group stayed in Basel in a schismatic and alternative Council (1439-1449) in which the Pope Eugene IV was deposed and the antipope Felix (+1451) was elected. Some relevant questions were debated in Basel: Conciliarism and the primacy of the Pope; the union with the Eastern Church; the question of the Immaculate Conception of the Virgin Mary.

[146] Debate on Eugene IV's legitimacy was brought to an end in 1448 when he was fully recognized by the German nation.

[147] Alonso García de Santa María had been an bachelor in Law by the University of Salamanca in 1405. He is also known as Alonso de Cartagena, to whom we will refer later. *Cf.* Vicente Beltrán de Heredia, «Castilla en el Concilio de Constanza» and «Personalidades castellanas en el Concilio de Basilea», in *Cartulario*, I, pp. 250-285 y 314-409.

[148] The University of Salamanca had to disaffirm some of its members. We keep a response of Pope Eugene IV to the University, which had written to condemn and disavow the conduct of its own envoy to the Council of Basel, Juan Alfonso de Segovia; Florence, January 25th 1441: *Bulario*, II, pp. 474-475.

[149] The Council of Basel was transferred to Ferrara in 1437 and to Florence in 1439.

[150] Eugene IV asked the University of Salamanca to send some doctors and masters to the Council of Ferrara, where they had moved from Basel; Bologna, September 23rd 1437: *Bulario*, II, pp. 428-429.

[151] Beltrán de Heredia, *Cartulario*, I, pp. 362-376. Apart from conciliarism, Juan de Segovia defended in Basel the Immaculate Conception of the Virgin Mary. Santiago Madrigal Terrazas, *El pensamiento eclesial de Juan de Segovia (1393-1458). La gracia en el tiempo*, Madrid, Universidad Pontificia de Comillas, 2004.

[152] Benigno Hernández Montes, *Biblioteca de Juan de Segovia. Edición y comentario de su escritura de donación*, Madrid, CSIC, 1984.

[153] Luis Fernández Gallardo, *Alonso de Cartagena. Una biografía política en la Castilla del siglo XV*, Valladolid, Junta de Castilla y León, 2002. Alonso de Cartagena (1385-1456) represents the epitome of the Christian humanism in the age of Juan II of Castile. He came from a family of converts in Burgos, and he ended up as Bishop of the city. He graduated in Laws by the University of Salamanca in 1405. From 1421, he was a member of the Royal Council. He was Ambassador in Portugal from 1421 to 1427, and Ambassador in the Council of Basel from 1434 to 1439; where he got in touch with other intellectuals of his time and with the Italian humanists. He translated Cicero and Seneca into Spanish, and he wrote works on ethics and political philosophy. One of his most important works is his *Discourse on the precedence of the Catholic King* [of Castile] *over the King of England* [*Discurso sobre la precedencia del Rey Católico sobre el de Inglaterra*], which was written in Basel. He also wrote other spiritual works and books in defense of New Christians or Converts. In 1424, Cartagena finished his translation of Cicero's *De inventione*, by request of the Prince Dom Duarte of Portugal. He decided to emphasize the importance of the contents over the form in the Rhetoric (of the *res* over the *verbum*), of the ideas expressed in the text over the imitation of the Classical language and syntax. Between 1434 and 1437 he argued with Bruni de Arezzo about Arezzo's translation of the *Nicomachean Ethics*. «Bruni defended a purist prose, he wanted to reach the pure Latin of the Classical authors, contrary to Cartagena, who was more ductile, and who asked for the exact word for each concept, be it

from Medieval Latin or contemporary Spanish»: Inmaculada Delgado Jara & Rosa M.ª Herrera García, «Humanidades y humanistas en la Universidad de Salamanca del siglo XV», in *Salamanca y su Universidad en el primer Renacimiento: siglo XV. Miscelánea Alfonso IX*, 2010, Salamanca, Ediciones Universidad de Salamanca, 2011, p. 257. In his *Discurso sobre la precedencia*, he defended a Spanish Monarchy that dated back to the pre-Roman ages, followed by the Goths, who created Spain and from which the Kings of Castile descended; and, at the same time, the Reconquista had provided the Kings of Spain with an incomparable hallmark of Catholicity: José M.ª Monsalvo Antón, «Poder y cultura en la Castilla de Juan II», p. 64.

[154] Court trajectory in the environment of Juan II, Henry IV and the Roman Curia.

[155] Isaac Vázquez Janeiro, «La Teología en el siglo XV», in *Historia de la Universidad de Salamanca. III-1. Saberes y confluencias*, Salamanca, Ediciones Universidad de Salamanca, 2006, pp. 184-187. Javier López de Goicoechea Zabala, *Dualismo cristiano y Estado moderno. Estudio histórico-crítico de la «Summa de Ecclesia» (1453) de Juan de Torquemada*, Salamanca, Universidad Pontificia, 2005.

[156] Juan Alfonso de Benavente, *Ars et doctrina studendi et docendi.* Critical edition by Bernardo Alonso Rodríguez, Salamanca, Universidad Pontificia de Salamanca, 1972, pp. 67-68. Salustiano de Dios, «Los juristas de Salamanca en el siglo XV», pp. 45-46.

[157] Master of Arts in 1426. Around 1430 he frequents the Studium Generale of San Francisco in Salamanca. He became a bachelor in Theology in 1432 and in Canons in 1434. He became a master of Theology in 1436-1441: Emiliano Fernández Vallina, «La importancia de Alfonso de Madrigal, el Tostado, Maestrescuela en la Universidad de Salamanca», in *Salamanca y su Universidad en el primer Renacimiento: siglo XV. Miscelánea Alfonso IX*, 2010, Salamanca, Ediciones Universidad de Salamanca, 2011, pp. 163-164.

[158] Florencio Marcos Rodríguez, «Los manuscritos de Alfonso de Madrigal conservados en la Biblioteca universitaria de Salamanca», *Salmanticensis*, 4 (Salamanca, 1957), pp. 3-50.

[159] Inmaculada Delgado Jara & Rosa M.ª Herrera García, «Humanidades y humanistas en la Universidad de Salamanca del siglo XV», in *Salamanca y su Universidad en el primer Renacimiento: siglo XV. Miscelánea Alfonso IX*, 2010, Salamanca, Ediciones Universidad de Salamanca, 2011, p. 258. José Manuel Sánchez Caro, Rosa M.ª Herrera & Inmaculada Delgado Jara, *Alfonso de Madrigal, el Tostado. Introducción al Evangelio según san Mateo*, Salamanca, Universidad Pontificia, 2008. El Tostado distinguishes the different meanings of the Scriptures in the *quaestio* 28 of the 13th Chapter of his *Commentary on the Gospel according to Saint Matthew*: «The first division is between the literal and the mystic sense, and the mystic interpretation is itself divided into three: allegorical, tropological and anagogical» («Prima divisio est in litteralem et mysticum et rursus mysticus dividitur in tres, allegoricus, tropologicus, anagogicus»). The literal sense is strictly textual: the words and their meaning (*per verba*). The allegorical sense refers to the figures, comparisons or anticipations, such as the ones in the Old Testament with regard to the New Testament. The tropological or moral sense clarifies the behaviors of the Christians. The anagogical sense refers to the symbols of the future life or the life that is anticipated with contemplation. *Cf.* Inmaculada Delgado Jara, «El Tostado y la exégesis bíblica», in *La primera Escuela de Salamanca (1406-1516)*, Salamanca, Ediciones Universidad de Salamanca, 2012, p. 66.

[160] Inmaculada Delgado Jara, «El Tostado y la exégesis bíblica», *op. cit.*, p. 60.

[161] «We must highlight El Tostado's inclination to the literal meaning of the Scriptures, to present a *litteralis* interpretation of the Bible, the only one valid for him when constructing the true Theology: «The Scriptures never state what is true or false in a mystical sense, but in the literal one», is what he said in the q. 28 of the *Commentary on the Gospel according to Saint Matthew*, 13, one of the texts which show more clearly the basis of his hermeneutics («Quia sensus mystici non probant»)»: Inmaculada Delgado Jara, «El Tostado y la exégesis bíblica», p. 64. Apart from Saint Thomas Aquinas, Nicholas of Lyra and Saint Jerome were also in favor of the literal exegesis of the Bible. The arguments of faith must come from literalness and not from symbols and allegories, in contrast with the Alexandrine tradition, which was originist, allegorical and mystical: «Theologia mystica non arguit».

[162] Emiliano Fernández Vallina, «La importancia de Alfonso de Madrigal», *op. cit.*, p.166.

[163] «El Tostado is not a complete humanist; his mind and his formal and structural expression are shaped according to the academic parameters [...]. His doctrine is not far from that of the Aristotelians-Thomists». «The humanist peculiarity of El Tostado is the importance he grants to Classical authors, the place they occupy in his arguments and the fact that he puts them on a level with sources from the Christian tradition»: Emiliano Fernández Vallina, «La importancia de Alfonso de Madrigal», *op. cit.*, pp. 169,170, 177. Nuria Belloso Martín, *Política y Humanismo en el siglo xv. El maestro Alfonso de Madrigal, el Tostado*, Valladolid, Universidad de Valladolid, 1989.

[164] «Some of his works already show a Renaissance style, such as his translations from Greek and Latin, the case of the translation of the *Church History* of Eusebius of Caesarea from Greek to Latin, or his books on mythological subjects, the *Treaty of the gods of the gentiles* [*Tratado de los dioses de la gentilidad*], or some of his works in Romance, such as his *Questions on moral Philosophy* [*Cuestiones sobre filosofía moral*], in which he presents the main moral virtues that appear in the second book of Aristotle's *Ethics* [...]. El Tostado tried to provide an innovation to the lectures with a Renaissance style by adding a preface, *prohemialis praelocutio*, which represented a variation with regard to the medieval discussions. This preface consisted of the introduction of a fable or a similar fiction, in which thanks to the richness of his classical erudition he digressed to the fields of mythology and ancient history before going back to the medieval structure of the scholastic dispute»: Inmaculada Delgado Jara & Rosa M.ª Herrera García, «Humanidades y humanistas en la Universidad de Salamanca del siglo xv», pp. 258-259.

[165] Inmaculada Delgado Jara, «El Tostado y la exégesis bíblica», pp. 59, 71.

[166] «When the 3rd Constitution of Benedict XIII of 1411 mentions the names of Avicenna and Arnaldus [de Villa Nova], it shows that, in all likelihood, their writings were the main basis of the *materia docendi* that was taught in the School [of Salamanca], maybe even since the end of the 14th century»: Marcelino V. Amasuno Sarraga, *La Escuela de Medicina...*, p. 151.

[167] Marcelino V. Amasuno Sarraga, p. 123. Luis García Ballester, «Galenismo y enseñanza médica en la Universidad de Salamanca del siglo xv», *Dynamis*, 20 (Granada, 2000), pp. 209-247.

[168] «The regime of Juan II tried to promote that cultural project in the Spanish language. The entire production associated to the court is written in Spanish, and there is a clear effort to transfer the Latin creations into Spanish [...]. A monarchy such as the Castilian one, albeit admitting and appreciating the Classical and humanist tradition, distorted it by adding it to

the academic corpus lacking its original language, and made the vernacular language grow stronger. That is the framework of the reception of Italian culture in Castile in the 15th century»: José M.ª Monsalvo Antón, «Poder y cultura en la Castilla de Juan II», p. 47.

[169] «Almost all the important intellectuals of their time came to the University of Salamanca. To take a case in point, two key figures, Juan de Mena and Alonso de Cartagena were educated in Salamanca. And many others: Juan de Torquemada (1388-1468), a great political thinker [...], an important figure who stood out in Basel and who entered the pontifical Curia; Juan de Cervantes (†1453), a Cardinal and Law graduate by the University of Salamanca who was another main figure of the great conciliar era; the canonists Juan González de Sevilla (†1440) and Juan Alfonso Mella (†1467); or the civilist Juan de Carvajal (†1469), member of the pontifical Curia and Cardinal; and Alfonso de la Torre (†1461), the first author of a moral treatise in Spanish, called *Delightful vision* [*Visión deleytable*], which was written in the decade of 1430 and is an example of Christian taxonomy and pre-Renaissance spirituality; and the jurist Díaz de Montalvo; or Clemente Sánchez de Verciel; and, of course, Rodrigo Sánchez de Arévalo (1404-1470), doctor in Civil Law and bachelor in Theology by the University of Salamanca, who was a diplomat in Basel in 1433-1439 before making the jump to Rome [...]; and even Pedro González de Mendoza, son of the Marquis of Santillana, who studied in Salamanca between 1446 and 1452, and who would later become Great Cardinal of Spain and a future patron of the Renaissance movement in the time of the Catholic Monarchs»: José M.ª Monsalvo Antón, «Poder y cultura en la Castilla de Juan II», pp. 70-71.

[170] That is, the «corpus iuris civilis et canonici», the Bible, the Sentences, Aristotle, Avicenna, etc: *Bulario*, I, p.175.

[171] *Bulario*, I, p. 173.

[172] *Bulario*, I, p. 171. There are inventories of the Library of San Bartolomé from around 1430: *Colegio Viejo de San Bartolomé (Salamanca). Inventario de bienes (siglo XV)*, Spanish manuscript 524 of the National Library of Paris. The Law section of this library has been assessed as follows: «According to what we can observe in the consecutive registers of the books of Law that are in the library of the College in those dates, around 1430 [...], the expert jurists of Salamanca must not have written much until that time, because in that period there was no book of Law in the Library from a Spanish author, except for those of Bernard of Compostella, and the only references to the Law of Castile were the *Peregrina*, the *Fuero Juzgo* and the *Fuero Real*, because all other works could be classified either as great sources of Canon law or Civil law, Decrees, Decretals, Codex, Volumen Legum and the different parts of the Digestum, together with collections and lists of glosses or practical works; or as works by renowned jurists who were experts in glosses and commentaries, civilists and cannonists, by Azo, Oldradus, Geoffrey of Trani, Huguccio, Petrus Jacobus, Bartolus, Baldus, Giovanni Faber, Cino, Innocentius, Zabarella, Guido de Baysio, Giovanni d'Andrea, Peter of Ancarano and Henry Hostiensis. This is, in any case, a most important testimony of the situation of Law teaching in Salamanca in the first decades of the 15th century, with a tendency towards European Common law but with the presence of the Royal law». *Cf.* Salustiano de Dios, «Los juristas de Salamanca en el siglo XV», pp. 30-31.

[173] Some noble families of Castile in the first half of the 15th century stored up books. That was the case of Rodrigo Alfonso Pimentel (1440-1461), Count of Benavente, who had family relations with the University of Salamanca. In the inventory of his library, which dates from 1440, we can find

around 120 manuscripts of chronicles, Latin classics, fine art, philosophy, falconry and medicine: *Bulario*, I, p. 174. The library of the Marquis of Santillana, Íñigo López de Mendoza (1398-1458), included several hundreds of books. The library of Álvaro de Stúñiga, Lord of Béjar, had 25 books in 1468. Pedro Fernández de Velasco, Count of Haro (1399-1470) had around 141 books in 1455. Fernán Pérez de Guzmán (†1460), uncle of the Marquis of Santillana, had about 185 volumes: José M.ª Monsalvo Antón, «Poder y cultura en la Castilla de Juan II», p. 84.

[174] «Reina, the Jewish librarian»: *Bulario*, I, p. 176.

[175] «The Cathedral appears as the richest institution of all, with the strongest estate and the highest and safest income»: José Luis Martín Martín, «Universidad y catedral en el Cuatrocientos salmantino», *op. cit.*, p. 101. The Cathedral probably outnumbered the University income by three to one. The Cathedral chapter was made up of around 54 benefice recipients, and the number rose to 67 at the end of the 15th century, not counting chaplains and servants. Apart from the tithe, the Cathedral chapter owned vast rural properties and 350 houses were owned or rented by it in the town of Salamanca at the end of the Middle Ages: *op. cit.*, pp. 96, 97, 102. All this estate of the Cathedral chapter was a good business for the sale and renting of houses and premises, and the houses for rent were occupied by lecturers and students in the University: *op. cit.*, pp. 106-107.

[176] We know that there is a commemorative inscription of the construction in Escuelas Mayores on the hallway of the Eastern door: «Year of the birth of Our Lord Jesus Christ of 1433, and the work began in the year 1415, and it was built by order of Antonio Ruiz de Segovia, doctor in Decrees, Maestrescuela of the Church of Salamanca, Chancellor of the University of the Studium of Salamanca by Apostolic Authority. The construction was built at the expense of the University of Salamanca by Alfonso Rodríguez Carpintero, master of the work. The administrator was Juan Fernández de Rágama, Precentor of Badajoz; and these were the professors of the Chairs of Sentences and Sciences that are taught in these Schools: Diego González, doctor in Laws; the Maestrescuela Juan González; Pedro Martínez; Juan Rodríguez, doctor in Decrees; Ferraz Rodríguez and Arias Maldonado, doctors in Laws; Brother Álvaro, Brother Lope and Juan González de Segovia, masters in Theology; Juan Ferrández, Gómez García, doctors in Medicine; and other lecturers. And the Chapel was built in the year [missing]»: *Historia de la Universidad de Salamanca hecha por el maestro Pedro Chacón (1569)*, edited by Ana M.ª Carabias Torres, Salamanca, Ediciones Universidad de Salamanca, 1990, pp. 45, 46. For its part, on April 28th 1429, Sancho, Bishop of Salamanca, had confirmed as the Chapel of the University «the house that had been built on the New Schools of the University of Salamanca in honor of Saint Jerome, which is located between the School of Decrees and the House of the Beadle»: Ángel Vaca Lorenzo, «Le campus de l'Université de Salamanque au Moyen Âge. Besoins fonctionnels et réponses inmobilières», in Patrick Gilli, Jacques Verger & Daniel Le Blévec, *Les universités et la ville au Moyen Âge*, Leiden-Boston, 2007, p. 43, footnote 100.

[177] «The choice of Saint [Saint Jerome] is perfectly in tune with his status in the University sphere, but we should also point out that maybe this choice also links him with Avignon because, as Daniel Russo suggests, its iconography as a Cardinal gains a renewed interest, and it is related to the importance of Cardinals within the hierarchy of the Church»: Lucía Lahoz, «La imagen de la Universidad de Salamanca en el Cuatrocientos», in *Salamanca y su Universidad en el primer Renacimiento: siglo XV. Miscelánea*

Alfonso IX, 2010, Salamanca, Ediciones Universidad de Salamanca, 2011, pp. 309-310. Daniel Russo, *Saint Jêrome en Italia, étude d'iconographie et de spiritualité, XIIIᵉ-XVIᵉ siècles,* Paris, 1987, pp. 51 onwards.

[178] Beltrán de Heredia, «La Universidad en el siglo xv», *Cartulario,* II, p. 198.

[179] Nieves Rupérez Almajano, *El Colegio Mayor de San Bartolomé o de Anaya.* Salamanca, Ediciones Universidad de Salamanca, 2003, p. 20. Nieves Ruipérez Almajano, «El Colegio de San Bartolomé antes de las reformas del siglo XVIII» in *Imagen, contextos morfológicos y universidades. Miscelánea Alfonso XI, 2012,* Salamanca, Ediciones Universidad de Salamanca, 2013, pp. 159-210.

[180] «The Studium of Salamanca is most noble and famous in your kingdom and abroad»: Cortes of Toledo of 1462, *Recopilaciones de Cortes,* III, p. 707. Cited by José M.ª Monsalvo Antón, «El Estudio y la ciudad en el período medieval…», p. 456.

[181] Fernando de Aragón visited Salamanca in May 1475 to look for supporters. Afterwards, the Catholic Monarchs stayed in the town from December 1486 until the end of January 1487.

[182] In March 1475, within the context of the Civil War, the mayor García Manrique appeared before the academic Senate and asked the University for a loan of 100,000 maravedís for the Crown. The rector complained that, according to the law, objects of gold and silver had to be left as a surety; but in the end he agreed to lend the money. *Cf.* Florencio Marcos Rodríguez, *Extractos de los Libros de Claustros de la Universidad de Salamanca. Siglo XV (1464-1481),* Salamanca, Universidad de Salamanca, 1964, pp. 209-210.

[183] In the meeting on March 16th 1478, a squire presented a letter from King Ferdinand in which he asked for a leave of absence for Doctor Andrés de Villalón, professor in the Vespers Chair of Laws «because the King is lacking lawyers». The majority of the representatives declined the leave: *Extractos,* p. 260.

[184] The progressive importance of the figure of the lawyer in Castile during the 15th century took shape in the Cortes of Toledo in 1480, where the Royal Council underwent a transformation and was now made up of a prelate, three noblemen and eight or nine lawyers. *Cortes de León y Castilla,* Madrid, Academia de la Historia, 1882, IV, pp. 111-112. *Cf.* Salustiano de Dios, *El Consejo Real de Castilla (1385-1522),* Madrid, Centro de Estudios Constitucionales, 1982. Lawyers increase their presence as collaborators of the King in the administrative and legal areas. The Catholic Monarchs promoted the study of Roman Civil law and Canon law «when they decided that those who wanted to carry out their duties in the field of justice had to study Canon or Civil law for at least ten years, that is, the necessary period to obtain a graduate degree, in the Universities of their Kingdoms, Salamanca and Valladolid»: Royal Order, Barcelona, July 6th 1493; Salustiano de Dios, «Los juristas de Salamanca en el siglo xv», p. 51. Lorenzo Galíndez de Carvajal talks about the concern of the Catholic Monarchs for the professional and intellectual training of their officers: «In order to be better prepared, they had a book with a list of those men with greater abilities and merits for vacant positions, and also for the allocation of Bishoprics and posts for ecclesiastical dignitaries»: Beltrán de Heredia, *Cartulario,* II, p. 23.

[185] Alexander VI notified the University of Salamanca that he had been elevated to the Papacy, and he asked for prayers to light his pontificate: Rome, August 26th 1492: Vicente Beltrán de Heredia, *Bulario de la*

Universidad de Salamanca (1219-1549), III, Salamanca, Universidad de Salamanca, 1967, p. 197.

[186] At the end of the conflict, Rodrigo Álvarez, Canon of Salamanca, was elected as the only Rector on March 18th 1480: *Extractos*, p. 306. This was a position for a dignitary from the Cathedral. Florencio Marcos Rodríguez, «Un cisma de rectores de la Universidad de Salamanca a fines del siglo XV», *Salmanticensis*, 14 (Salamanca, 1967), pp. 341-369.

[187] Vicente Beltrán de Heredia, *Cartulario de la Universidad de Salamanca. La Universidad en el Siglo de Oro*, II, Salamanca, Universidad de Salamanca, 1970, pp. 133-134. Even the Catholic Monarchs, the King and Queen of Castile, behaved as «patrons of an ecclesiastical centre». *Cf.* M.ª Paz Alonso Romero, «El fuero universitario, siglos XIII-XIX», *op. cit.*, p. 168.

[188] Beltrán de Heredia, *Bulario*, I, p. 189. Bull of Rome, August 1st 1497: *Bulario*, III, pp. 201-202.

[189] «Ever since the Capitulations, it was understood that the figure of the Maestrescuela represented a double nature of pontifical and Royal judge: pontifical for clergymen and Royal for laymen». *Cf.* M.ª Paz Alonso Romero, «El fuero universitario», *op. cit.*, p. 171.

[190] The question of the territorial limits of the jurisdiction of the Maestrescuela is a complex one. As an apostolic custodian by appointment of Eugene IV since 1431, it spread to four *dietas* around Salamanca. The Catholic Monarchs confirmed this distance in the Capitulations of 1492, but they reduced it to only two *dietas* in 1494. The result was that the area of action of the Maestrescuela reached four *dietas* when he acted as a pontifical custodian and only two *dietas* when he acted as a Royal custodian. *Cf.* M.ª Paz Alonso Romero, «El fuero universitario», *op. cit.*, p. 177. A *dieta* was defined as the distance that could be covered on foot in a day, about ten leagues in total, and each league was made up of three miles.

[191] Esperabé, I, p. 122-124. Royal Order, Toledo, May 4th 1480: «Some noblemen and squires and other people, ecclesiastics as well as laymen, neighbours of the town and from abroad, have meddled in the past and still do it every time that a Chair is vacant or that any other position in the University needs to be filled. And they try to appoint people who are not suitable for these jobs, and to do it they bribe the officers and other people from the Studium, and they implore and beg and threat, and they look for different ways to convince them to give them their votes, with exquisite gifts and promises and coercion. All this means that these positions are occupied against the norms and dispositions established in the Constitutions and statutes of the University».

[192] This was declared in the Cortes of Toledo of 1462, *Cortes*, III, p. 708. *Cf.* José María Monsalvo Antón, «La sociedad concejil de los siglos XIV y XV. Caballeros y pecheros (en Salamanca y en Ciudad Rodrigo)», in José Luis Martín Rodríguez & José M.ª Mínguez (eds.), *Historia de Salamanca*, II, Salamanca, Centro de Estudios Salmantinos, 1997, pp. 389-478.

[193] We can find one example of the lack of urban safety caused by the clashes between different factions in the Senate on November 21st 1474: «Doctor Martín de Ávila came before us and stated his natural fear of coming to teach his lectures, which he could not do without putting himself in danger, due to his enmity with Pedro Suárez de Solís [...]. And he was afraid because his relatives, who had sided with the group of San Benito, had fled the city, and his enemies could walk freely around the place, which entailed a grave danger for him». *Cf.* Florencio Marcos Rodríguez, *Extractos de los Libros de Claustros de la Universidad de Salamanca. Siglo XV (1464-1481)*, *op. cit.*, p. 203.

[194] We follow the classification proposed by Antonio García y García: «Consolidaciones del siglo xv», p. 44. And also the remarks of Mariano Peset & Pilar García Trobat, «Poderes y modelos universitarios, siglos xv-xix», *op. cit.*, pp. 48 onwards.

[195] The papal Constitutions established that the representatives were elected by the general assembly of the University corporation.

[196] «The Cathedral chapter and the University in the 15th century represented the two main income and power hubs of the town [...], they complemented each other, and some of the most influential figures of the century in Salamanca based the promotion of their careers on these institutions»: José Luis Martín Martín, «Universidad y catedral en el Cuatrocientos salmantino», in *Salamanca y su Universidad en el primer Renacimiento: siglo xv. Miscelánea Alfonso IX, 2010*, Salamanca, Ediciones Universidad de Salamanca, 2011, p. 117.

[197] There are different lineages from Salamanca who were involved in positions of the Cathedral chapter and the University alike: The house of Bonal, since the second half of the 14th century; the Camargo family and the Castilla family, since the first half of the 15th century; the Vivero family, since the second half of the 15th century... Among the members of these connected families we can find Bishops, Maestrescuelas, Canons, Rectors of the University, Professors, University representatives, graduates, town mayors, etc. *Cf.* José Luis Martín Martín, «Universidad y catedral en el Cuatrocientos salmantino», *op. cit.*, pp. 107-116.

[198] José Luis Martín Martín defends this thesis in his work «El Archivo de la catedral y la Historia de la Universidad de Salamanca», pp. 37-45. He studied the period 1464-1480, and he found that, out of the 56 Prebendaries of the Cathedral, half of them also occupied a position in the University. The author points out that at least eight of these Prebendaries became Rectors and another twelve were Vice-rectors (p. 42). In the group of Prebendaries who became Rectors there are two Archdeacons, two Precentors, three Canons and one minor Canon. There were other University posts occupied by Prebendaries, such as primicerius, representative, counselor and accountant. The author adds: «All this makes it advisable to qualify the rigid statements that were previously held, such as the student status of Rectors and Vice-rectors» (p. 44). The *student* who was also a Rector and a Prebendary was fully solvent, had connections and a certain maturity; it was a high-rank *student*.

[199] As Bernardo Alonso Rodríguez had already pointed out in «Las Escuelas de Cánones del Estudio salmantino en la Edad Media», p. 470.

[200] «The Archive's characteristics are similar to those of other medieval archives in the same area: external documents at first and a progressive presence of its own documents when the institution has matured and is spreading, which means the multiplication of the bureaucratic procedures»: Miguel Ángel Jaramillo Guerreira, «Documentación medieval en el Archivo universitario salmantino», p. 341. «The disappearance of documentes which were signed by the different notaries who worked in the Studium during the 15th century and the first half of the 16th century runs in line with what happened in all the registries of Castile in that time. The lack of documents is due to the fact that these notaries considered the documents as their own»: *ibidem*, p. 342.

[201] Enrique Esperabé Arteaga, *Historia pragmática e interna de la Universidad de Salamanca. II. Maestros y alumnos más distinguidos*, Salamanca, Librería Núñez Izquierdo, 1917, pp. 243-244. The temporary Chairs were assigned by the board of the Rector and his counselors with

a previous application or examination. When the academic year 1464-1465 started, the bachelor Diego de Benavente applied as a candidate for the temporary Terce Chair of Canons: «He stated that this bachelor was applying for the Chair and he asked for a celebratory meal to be held and for him to take up the Chair. And after discussing this among them, they agreed to grant him the Chair». *Cf.* Beltrán de Heredia, «La Universidad en el siglo XV», p. 224.

[202] Esperabé, II, pp. 244-245.

[203] Esperabé, II, pp. 245-246.

[204] Esperabé, II, pp. 246-247.

[205] Esperabé, II, pp. 247-248.

[206] There are no references to the temporary Chairs of Medicine until May 8th 1465: *Libros de Claustros*, 1, fol. 50r. Florencio Marcos, *Extractos*, p. 73: The bachelor Gabriel Álvarez Abarca, son of Fernán Álvarez Malla, who was the first doctor of the Queen, applied for a temporary Chair.

[207] Esperabé, II, p. 248. Several bachelors in charge of the classrooms were appointed by the board of the Rector and his counselors due to the large influx of students. There is a reference to this large amount of scholars in the minutes of March 15th 1473, which report an audience of 150 students in a class of Grammar. Among these temporary Chairs of Grammar and repeated lessons there was a Psalter Chair which appeared between 1466 and 1530. Also, and with permission of the Rector and his counselors «other lessons were repeated outside the classrooms or in premises nearby». *Cf.* Beltrán de Heredia, «La Universidad en el siglo XV», pp. 220, 226.

[208] Esperabé, II, pp. 248-249.

[209] In the meeting on December 14th 1478 there is a conflict of competences and interests among all these teachers. Those who repeated the lessons and were not officially appointed managed to read them inside the Escuelas Menores building, as had been the custom in the last thirty or forty years. *Cf. Libros de Claustros*, 3, fols. 37-38; and Beltrán de Heredia, «La Universidad en el siglo XV», p. 227.

[210] Manuscript 210 of the Library of the University of Salamanca, fol. 21 and 31. Beltrán de Heredia, *Cartulario*, II, p. 228, points out: «Afterwards, this became general practice for all those who worked by appointment of the Senate or the Rector and his counselors, and even for some individuals when they covered the hours in which the masters did not attend their regulated lessons».

[211] The collections are mentioned in the minute books of the Senate meetings *Libros de Claustros*, 1, fol. 71v, of the year 1466. According to University historian Pedro Chacón, collections were suspended in 1480 and lectures in exchange for money were also cancelled: «It was the year of 1480, and the number of students and the income from the Tercias grew considerably, although at that time there were 25 main Chairs in all the fields of science and another large amount of lessons and temporary Chairs occupied by bachelors, who could not become graduates without teaching for four years first, according to the Constitutions, some of which wanted to occupy the main Chairs that were left vacant. The University established the creation of lesser Chairs in all the faculties and for them to be paid from the coffers of the Studium in order to provide for the erudite men who were in the University. Therefore, when the main Chairs were left vacant, the students would be aware of the merits and abilities of each of these men, so that they could choose the one that they preferred». *Cf. Historia de la Universidad de Salamanca hecha por el maestro Pedro Chacón (1569),* edited

by Ana M.ª Carabias, Salamanca, Ediciones Universidad de Salamanca, 1990, pp. 95-96.

[212] That was the case, for example, in the examination for the Vespers Chair of Medicine in 1469. The candidate was the graduate Forés, who was very popular among the students. The examination took place in the Senate meeting on July 20th 1469: «Let the students of Medicine know that they have to come and vote after the examination has taken place, and that no candidate can be in the premises, and that they cannot bring men or ecclesiastics, armed or unarmed, into the premises or in the neighboring streets, so that the students are free to vote»: *Libros de Claustros*, 1, fol. 164v; *Extractos*, p. 131. The position was granted to Forés (1469-1478), who was rather unreliable and was constantly absent from his lessons. Forés was a court doctor for the Bishop Gonzalo de Vivero and Alonso I de Fonseca, Archbishop of Seville: Marcelino V. Amasuno Sarrago, *La Escuela de Medicina*, pp. 87, 91.

[213] Rome, October 1st 1489: *Bulario*, III, p. 191-192.

[214] *Libros de Claustros*, 3, fol. 36.

[215] The lack of minute books or *Libros de Claustros* from that time (1481-1502) in the University Archive (AUSA) makes it impossible to be more specific.

[216] «There were different factions among the students, and they had even fought with cudgels and hurled abuse at each other. This led to a great disturbance and there were attempts to put an end to the situation, because students did no longer study, and they only discussed about their masters even before the Chairs were left vacant»: Minutes of the Senate meeting on January 3rd 1504, in *Libros de Claustros*, 4, fol. 105v. However, from April 1511, the students voted for the holders of the temporary Chairs, just like in the tenured Chairs: *Libros de Claustros*, 5, fols. 323v-324. *Cf.* Beltrán de Heredia, *Cartulario*, II, pp. 230, 231.

[217] Beltrán de Heredia, *Cartulario*, II, pp. 233-234. The consolidation of temporary Chairs which were occupied for one academic year at the end of the 15th century meant that the official educational system was divided into two levels: tenured Chairs and temporary Chairs; plus a third level of bachelors and trainees or subordinates. Apart from bachelors, graduates usually stood in for tenured professors when they were absent. These graduates were temporary substitutes who were elected by the votes of the students.

[218] Beltrán de Heredia, *Bulario*, I, p. 184.

[219] Beltrán de Heredia, *Cartulario*, II, p.53.

[220] For the review and passing of their academic degrees, those who had graduated outside the Studium Generale from 1464 had to present their degrees before the Board within three months: Cortes of Toledo of 1480, IV, Madrid, Academia de la Historia, 1882, p. 183.

[221] One way to graduate with fewer costs and requirements was to ask for a dispensation not to take all the compulsory years, or to graduate outside the Studium of Salamanca with a rigged examining board. A bull by Innocent VIII from Rome, January 18th 1487, established that in the Kingdoms of León and Castile, those who graduated outside a Studium Generale would not obtain the privileges of those who graduated inside it, and that poor students could take their exams for free. However, some students still received their degrees outside the Studium, with the same privileges, by authorization of the Popes and with the acquiescence of the Monarchs: *Bulario*, I, p. 188 and *Bulario*, III, pp. 183-185.

[222] «The clerics had more opportunities to fund their studies and to find a job at the service of the Church»: Antonio García y García, «Consolidaciones del siglo xv», p. 55. Mariano Peset & Juan Gutiérrez Cuadrado, «Clérigos y juristas en la Baja Edad Media castellano-leonesa», *Senara*, 3 (Vigo, 1981), Appendix 1, pp. 7-110. On November 15th 1466, in the Prime Chair of Medicine of Doctor Fernán Álvarez de Mella, there were 20 students in the class: *Libros de Claustros*, 1, fol. 86v. In Grammar, however, up to 150 students could be found in a classroom in the year 1473, *cf.* Beltrán de Heredia, «La Universidad en el siglo xv», pp. 220 onwards.

[223] *Cartulario*, II, p. 40. The student population in 1504 was between 2,500 and 3,000 people «including doctors and masters and officers and students and other people from this same Studium»: Archivo General de Simancas, Cámara de Castilla, Pueblos (Salamanca), leg. 16: Census. *Cf.* José Luis Martín Martín, «Estructura demográfica y profesional de Salamanca a finales de la Edad Media», *Salamanca. Revista de Estudios*, 1 (Salamanca, 1982), pp. 15-33.

[224] José M.ª Monsalvo Antón, «El Estudio y la ciudad en el período medieval», p. 457.

[225] On July 14th 1479, all lectures and lessons are suspended until the day of Saint Luke, in October, due to the plague epidemic that had been declared in the town: *Libros de Claustros*, 3, fol. 85r; *Extractos*, p. 290. The plague was still active in December, and it killed five members of the teaching staff: professors of the Vespers Chair of Canons, Prime Chair of Grammar, Natural Physics and Singing/Music. *Cf.* Marcelino V. Amasuno, *La Escuela de Medicina...*, *op. cit.*, p. 84.

[226] *Cartulario*, II, pp. 50, 57.

[227] A bull authorized students from the College of San Bartolomé of Salamanca to reform their Constitutions; Rome, August 21st 1469: *Bulario*, III, pp. 134-135. The medieval documents from the College of San Bartolomé are now lost, although we know that its archives contained more than 130 documents dated before 1500: Miguel Ángel Jaramillo, «Documentación medieval...», p. 339.

[228] Renewal of the privileges granted to the students from the College of San Bartolomé of Salamanca to graduate with reduced costs; Rome, October 19th 1491: *Bulario*, III, pp. 195-196.

[229] In the Senate meeting on June 3rd 1479, the members of the board agreed to ask Pedro González de Mendoza, Cardinal since 1473, not to found it in Valladolid: «Because doing it here will benefit and honor the University»: *Libros de Claustros*, 3, fol. 78r; *Extractos*, p. 286.

[230] Request to the Archdeacon of Ledesma for an authorization for students in the Halls of Pan y Carbón to continue in the Halls after they are promoted to bachelors, as was the case of the College of San Bartolomé, Rome, March 9th 1501: *Bulario*, III, pp. 206-207. The medieval documents from the Halls of Pan y Carbón (founded around 1386) was transferred to the Archives of the current Pontifical University of Salamanca: Luis Sala Balust, *Catálogo de fuentes para la historia de los antiguos colegios seculares de Salamanca*, Madrid-Barcelona, Instituto Enrique Flórez, 1954, pp. 51-53.

[231] «In the time of the Catholic Monarchs, the following people were Counselors of Castile [and students from the Halls of San Bartolomé]: Diego de Villalpando, Lope de Ágreda, Tomás Cuenca, (Juan Alonso de Mogrovejo did not accept the post), Pedro González de Fontiveros, Alonso Rodríguez de Villaescusa, Francisco de Malpartida, Pedro Oropesa, Diego Villamuriel, Juan López de Palacios Rubios, Sancho de Frías, Juan de la Fuente, Garci-Ibáñez de Múxica, Toribio Gómez de Santiago, Miguel

Guerrero, Gonzalo Yáñez de Castro, Alonso Polo and Gaspar Montoya»: Ana M.ª Carabias Torres, «Colegios Mayores y letrados, 1406-1516», p. 31. Students from the College of San Bartolomé (also called *bartolomicos* or *bartolomeos*) who were raised to the episcopal dignity in this period were: «Tello de Buendía, Juan Arias Dávila, Pedro Jiménez de Préxamo, Diego Ramírez de Villaescusa, his older brother Gil or García Ramírez de Villaescusa, Diego Ortiz de Calzadilla, Francisco Sánchez de la Fuente, Gonzalo de Villadiego, Juan Ruiz de Medina, Alonso de Madrigal (El Tostado), Alonso Manso, Pedro de Parco, Francisco de Herrera and Íñigo López de Mendoza; who would later be followed by the Archbishop of Seville, Fernando de Valdés, an important prelate from the Empire. Tello de Buendía was a tutor of the Prince Juan, and Pedro de Oropesa was master of Alonso de Aragón (Archbishop of Aragón and son of Ferdinand the Catholic)»: *ibidem*, p. 32. «Above this [episcopal] dignity, the number of students becomes thinner, because the highest ecclesiastical positions were traditionally reserved for the nobility. Nevertheless, there were some *bartolomeos*, such as Juan de Mella, the first Cardinal who came from a Hall of Residence, in 1456; Francisco Herrera, Archbishop of Granada; Íñigo López de Mendoza y Zúñiga (his great-grandfather was the Marquis of Santillana), who was Archbishop of Burgos and was promoted to Cardinal; Gonzalo Maldonado, Archbishop of Tarragona; Pedro de Oropesa, Archbishop of Toledo and governor of Castile; and Fernando de Valdés, Archbishop of Seville, apart from General Inquisitor and member of the Council of State»: *ibidem*, p. 32. Reports were asked for in order to prepare lists of people with merits to enter the Administration. There is one report from the years 1496-1497 about «some erudite, noble and good people who are now in Salamanca». 25 students are recommended: ten from Canon law, six from Arts and Theology, five from Civil law, two unspecified scholars and two from Medicine. There is a predominance of Ecclesiastical Sciences; although the document was addressed to the Archbishop of Toledo, Cisneros: Beltrán de Heredia, *Cartulario*, II, pp. 163-164.

²³² Luis Sala Balust, *Constituciones, estatutos y ceremonias de los colegios seculares…*, I, pp. 73-77. In October 1498, Juan Gutiérrez, bachelor in Canons, was stripped of his condition of member of the College of San Bartolomé because it was discovered that he descended from Jews: Buenaventura Delgado, *El Colegio de San Bartolomé de Salamanca. Privilegios, bienes, pleitos, deudas y catálogo biográfico de colegiales*, Salamanca, Ediciones Universidad de Salamanca, 1986, p. 93.

²³³ «The University of Salamanca from the 15ᵗʰ century is mainly a medieval University, preceding the Renaissance Humanism. There are some humanist glimpses right at the end of the century and they come from outside […]. Jurists feel comfortable inside the system of the medieval Common-Roman-Canon law»: Antonio García y García, «Consolidaciones del siglo XV», p. 51. «Humanism in the 15ᵗʰ century, which has been extensively studied by specialists on Language and Literature, or Philosophy, or even Theology, does not seem to have had much of an influence on the mind of these jurists from Salamanca. When they wrote about Law, instead of about other subjects that were not strictly legal-related, they kept in line with the more traditional ways of interpreting the Law»: Salustiano de Dios, «Los juristas de Salamanca en el siglo XV», p. 18.

²³⁴ Bernardo Alonso Rodríguez, *Juan Alfonso de Benavente. Canonista salmantino del siglo XV*, Roma/Madrid, CSIC, 1964. Juan Alfonso de Benavente, *Ars et Doctrina Studendi et Docendi*. Critical edition by Bernardo

Alonso Rodríguez, Salamanca, Universidad Pontificia de Salamanca, 1972 [work written in 1453].

[235] Antonio García y García, «Juristas salmantinos, siglos XIV-XV. Manuscritos e impresos», *op. cit.*, p. 122. They mainly taught during the second half of the 15th century: Esperabé, II, pp. 242-243. Salustiano de Dios, «Los juristas de Salamanca en el siglo XV», pp. 41-42.

[236] «They are the unequivocal sign of the promotion received by Law studies in Salamanca since the last third of the 15th century and an advance of what would come next»: Salustiano de Dios, «Los juristas de Salamanca en el siglo XV», p. 18.

[237] Salustiano de Dios, «Los juristas de Salamanca en el siglo XV», p. 52: «The criticism by the grammarian Elio Antonio de Nebrija [...] reveals the situation of Law studies in Salamanca at that time, which closely followed the methods of scholastic dialectics, obsessed with arguing, convincing and concluding around a certain question or case, leaving aside the Latin texts and the establishment of a context, which were not particularly important aspects to the mind of these legal specialists». And from the same author and work: «Legal humanism, with its thirst for brevity and order in the exhibition of arguments, accuracy in the definitions and the elements of the institutions, criticism on the abuse of authority quotes, purity of Latin and historical sense, came relatively late to Salamanca, after the decade of 1530, and it would stay there until the middle of the 17th century».

[238] Salustiano de Dios, «Los juristas de Salamanca en el siglo XV», pp. 55-56. Florencio Marcos Rodríguez, «La antigua biblioteca de la catedral de Salamanca», *Revista Hispania Sacra*, 14 (Madrid, 1961), pp. 281-319

[239] Salustiano de Dios, «Los juristas de Salamanca en el siglo XV», p. 59: «As an example, they had the Pope, who was undoubtedly above the Council».

[240] Salustiano de Dios, «Los juristas de Salamanca en el siglo XV», pp. 65-68.

[241] Papal confirmation (Sixtus IV) of the sentence passed in Alcalá by the Archbishop of Toledo Alfonso Carrillo against the master Pedro Martínez de Osma; Rome, August 9th 1446: *Bulario*, III, pp. 164-166. The apostolic bull against these doctrines that were contrary to the faith seems to refer to a circle of followers from the University: «Iniquitatis filii». José Labajos Alonso, *Proceso contra Pedro de Osma*, Salamanca, Universidad Pontificia de Salamanca, 2010.

[242] The books were burnt in front of the entrance of the Canon building of the Escuelas Mayores, and although some proposed to burn the Chair of master Osma, they did not do it in the end: «In Salamanca, Tuesday, 15 days into the month of June of the year 79, the entire University was summoned on pain of *prestiti juramenti* by the Rector and on pain of excommunication by the Maestrescuela. Everyone gathered in the Chapel of San Jerónimo from the chapters and the Escuelas Mayores of the Studium of Salamanca, and a Mass of the Holy Spirit was offered. Master Brother Juan de Santispíritus preached on the pulpit [...], and at the end of the sermon, in full view of the doctors and masters and graduates and bachelors and students of the Studium, he handed certain books and volumes from the treatise *De Confesione*, by master Osma and his supporters, to Diego de Villafátima, bailiff of the Maestrescuela, to burn them. He declared that he gave the books to him on behalf of the University, which obeyed and abided by the apostolic commandments that the Archbishop of Toledo had given to the University [...]. The bailiff received the books and started a fire in front of the doors of the Canon building of the Escuelas Mayores in the presence

of the entire University, and he threw the books into the fire, which burned them until they became nothing but ashes»: *Libros de Claustros*, 3, fol. 77v; *Extractos*, p. 286. Afterwards, towards 1569, in the first book on the History of the University by master Pedro Chacón, this event was narrated as follows: «A master and a great erudite came from another University [Master Pedro de Osma] to teach in a Chair of Theology in Salamanca, and in his lectures he established a new opinion regarding confession and the authority of the Pope, and he was so convinced of his theory that he even printed it later. The University organized a solemn procession on a certain day and summoned all the members of the Studium, and the buildings of the Escuelas were purified with holy ceremonies. A Mass of the Holy Spirit and a sermon were then offered in the chapel of the University, in order to condemn the theories of the books. Once that the service had ended, in the middle of the courtyard and in the presence of all, the University ordered to burn the Chair in which the theories had been exposed and the books in which they were written, and nobody left until everything had turned into ashes»: *Historia de la Universidad de Salamanca, hecha por el maestro Pedro Chacón, op. cit.*, pp. 103-104.

[243] *In Simbolum quicumque*, 1472-1474?; a coursebook on the Catholic faith made at the request of Juan Árias Dávila, Bishop of Segovia. «For Pedro de Osma, the *Summa Theologica* was the text that took over from the *Sentences* of Peter Lombard [...]. Pedro de Osma orients his lectures towards a return to the safe authors: Aristotle and Saint Thomas Aquinas. He wanted to restore them as a way to solve the problems of the Renaissance and to establish a solid and safe doctrine»: José Luis Fuertes Herreros, «Pensamiento y Filosofía en la Universidad de Salamanca del siglo xv», in *Salamanca y su Universidad en el primer Renacimiento: siglo XV. Miscelánea Alfonso IX*, 2010, Salamanca, Ediciones Universidad de Salamanca, 2011, p. 214 y 220.

[244] José Labajos Alonso, «Pedro de Osma y Fernando de Roa: significación histórica», in Cirilo Flórez Miguel et al., *La primera Escuela de Salamanca (1406-1516)*, Salamanca, Ediciones Universidad de Salamanca, 2012, pp. 161-162. This same importance of Thomism can be seen in the works of his disciple, Fernando de Roa, professor in the Prime Chair of Theology since 1494.

[245] Isaac Vázquez Janeiro, «La Teología en el siglo xv», *op. cit.*, p. 192. «As a theologian, Pedro de Osma is now seen as a reformer of the scholastic method, because he based his theses on the life of the Old Church, the Patristics and the Councils [...]. A Christian, theological and ecclesial humanist»: Inmaculada Delgado Jara & Rosa M.ª Herrera García, «Humanidades y humanistas en la Universidad de Salamanca del siglo xv», p. 260.

[246] The correction and amendment of some biblical texts was entrusted to him by the Cathedral chapter of Salamanca. «It seems that this interest on the biblical hermeneutics that is assumed in him comes from afar; probably from his studies in Osma, his original diocese, in which different Jewish communities had settled and created cultural centers which studied the Scriptures»: José Labajos Alonso, «Pedro de Osma y Fernando de Roa», p. 148.

[247] Esperabé, II, p. 247, 301. Marcelino V. Amasuno Sarraga, *La Escuela de Medicina*, p. 80.

[248] Antón Rodríguez de Salamanca is praised by Lucio Marineo Sículo among the teachers of Arts: «Primus et emeritus est magister Antonius [Roderici de Salamanca], philosophus medicusque doctissimus, qui

plurimum quodque et eloquentia claret»: *De Hispaniae laudibus*, Burgos, 1497.

[249] Books of Natural Philosophy and Medicine were included in the University Library in August 18th 1472: «In the Library of the Studium, they put the books to the left of the chest. There was a compilation of texts on Natural Philosophy and another on Logic, and some questions by Juan Canónygo on the *De generatione*; and on the shelf of Medicine they put a *Viaticum* by Constantine together with many other treatises and another book by Galen, *De ingenyo sanitatis*, and *De rregimine acutorum*, with many treatises and books by Bernardus Gordonius and other questions by Buridan on the *Physics*»: *Libros de Claustros*, 1, fol. 229r; *Extractos*, p. 169.

[250] Antonio García y García, «Consolidaciones del siglo xv», *op. cit.*, p. 52. In his dialogue about the foundations of Philosophy, written between 1474 and 1479, Osma proposed a distancing from the nominalists.

[251] Aristotle's medieval knowledge was centered on the Logic; and the most widely used textbook in the universities was the *Summulae logicales* (1270) by Petrus Hispanus. «Knowledge about the rest of his [Aristotle's] philosophical works started in Salamanca with Pedro de Osma and his commentary to the last six books of the *Metaphysics*, written around 1457, with the commentary to the books of the *Nicomachean Ethics* (1460) and the commentary to the books of the *Politics* (1460-1463)»: José Labajos Alonso, «Pedro de Osma y Fernando de Roa», pp. 152-153. This appreciation of Aristotle is shared by his disciple, Fernando de Roa, professor of Moral Philosophy in the year 1473-1474, who explained in his classes the commentaries of his master and prepared their edition. Osma's teaching methodology with regard to Aristotle started with the enunciation of the subject that was going to be dealt with followed by the concepts and opinions and finally the conclusions, with the counterarguments and the answer to the objections. Pedro Martínez de Osma, *Comentario a la Ética de Aristóteles*. Critical edition by José Labajos Alonso, Salamanca, Universidad Pontificia de Salamanca, 1996. Pedro de Osma & Fernando de Roa, *Comentario a la Política de Aristóteles*. Edited by José Labajos Alonso, Salamanca, Universidad Pontificia de Salamanca, 2006, 2 vols.

[252] Pedro de Osma knows and uses the direct versions of Aristotle's works prepared by the Italian humanists. Particularly, he used the translation of the *Nicomachean Ethics* (1418) and the books of the *Politics* (1435) that were translated from Greek into Latin by Leonardo Bruni. «There was a reunion with the humanist Aristotle, the Aristotle who was discovered and advocated by Leonardo Bruni, who was followed and made known in Salamanca by Alonso de Cartagena [...]. This version of Aristotle is present in the work by Pedro de Osma, who used Bruni's version of the *Nicomachean Ethics*»: José Luis Fuertes Herreros, «Pensamiento y Filosofía en la Universidad de Salamanca del siglo xv», pp. 216-217. José Labajos Alonso, «Pedro de Osma, impulsor del Humanismo y del conocimiento de Aristóteles en Salamanca», *Cuadernos Salmantinos de Filosofía*, 22 (Salamanca, 1995), pp. 135-158. Osma is opposed to the verbosity of Dialectics. He is against the syllogisms, subtleties and abstractions and promotes the specific terms of the Rhetoric. He defends that moral and political explanations can be better expressed through Rhetoric; and that Logic belongs with the speculative sciences. He is also concerned about grammatical purity, as can be seen in his clear support to Antonio de Nebrija when he took the examination for hte Chair of Grammar of Salamanca in January 1476: *Libros de Claustros*, 2, fol. 73.

253 «It seems that his commentary on the *Quicumque* was the first work to be produced in the printing press of Juan Parix [de Segovia]»: José Labajos Alonso, «Pedro de Osma y Fernando de Roa», p. 150. We have seen that Pedro de Osma has a good knowledge of the Aristotelian corpus, and so do his main commentators: Averroes, Avicenna, Albertus Magnus. But his works and commentaries include other quotes and authorities: ancient philosophers (Plato, Boethius); classical authors (Cicero, Seneca, Lactantius, Virgil); Fathers of the Church (St. Augustine, St. Jerome, St. Gregory); medieval theologians (Dionysius the Areopagite, St. Isidore, Peter Lombard, St. Thomas); the Holy Scriptures (Old and New Testaments); legal quotes (Digestum, Decrees, Decretals): José Labajos Alonso, «Pedro de Osma y Fernando de Roa», pp. 153, 154, 160.

254 It is already mentioned in the Constitutions of 1411.

255 Esperabé, II, p. 249.

256 In San Bartolomé there was a library with a section of science and astronomy. There are references for the purchase of books on Alchemy, Astrology, Physics, Arithmetic, Logic, etc. at the end of the 15th century: Guy Beaujouan, *Manuscrits scientifiques médiévaux de l'Université de Salamanque et de ses «Colegios Mayores»*, Bordeaux, Féret et Fils, 1962, pp. 20-24.

257 Cirilo Flórez Miguel, «Las ciencias y la Universidad de Salamanca en el siglo xv», in *Salamanca y su Universidad en el primer Renacimiento: siglo XV. Miscelánea Alfonso IX*, 2010, Salamanca, Universidad de Salamanca, 2011, p. 181. Cirilo Flórez Miguel et al., *La ciencia del cielo. Astrología y Filosofía natural en la Universidad de Salamanca (1450-1530)*, Salamanca, Caja de Ahorros y Monte de Piedad, 1989.

258 José Chabás & Bernard R. Goldstein, *Abraham Zacut (1452-1515) y la Astronomía en la península ibérica*, Salamanca, Ediciones Universidad de Salamanca, 2009.

259 «It was a planetary painted on the ceiling of the Library as if it were a great book of Nature, whose main objective is the practical teaching of Astrology [...]. The starts painted in it have a scientific basis on the list of stars of Zacut's works»: Cirilo Flórez Miguel, «Las ciencias y la Universidad de Salamanca en el siglo xv», *op. cit.*, pp. 187-188. P. Silva Maroto, *Fernando Gallego*, Salamanca, Caja Duero, 2004.

260 José Luis Espinel Marcos & Ramón Hernández Martín, *Colón en Salamanca: los dominicos*, Salamanca, Caja de Ahorros y Monte de Piedad, 1988. Eugenio García Zarza (coord.), «Salamanca y Colón». Monográfico en *Salamanca. Revista de Estudios*, n.º 54 (Salamanca, 2006).

261 «The geometrical theory of proportions and the experience of seafarers are going to be expressed within the classrooms of the University of Salamanca in a global image of the Earth, which goes beyond the closed and limited space with the look of the *ecumene* and opens a new global space of the Earth as the new space of modernity. All events in Human History will now have to be reconstructed and relocated, because they are no longer put in relation to the Mediterranean, but to the entire globe»: Cirilo Flórez Miguel, «Las ciencias y la Universidad de Salamanca en el siglo xv», *op. cit.*, p. 198.

262 Esperabé, II, pp. 248, 309, 315, 264-267. Félix G. Olmedo, *Nebrija en Salamanca (1475-1513)*, Madrid, Editora Nacional, 1944. Francisco Rico, *Nebrija frente a los bárbaros*, Salamanca, Universidad de Salamanca, 1978. Víctor García de la Concha (dir.), *Nebrija y la introducción del Renacimiento en España*, Salamanca, Universidad de Salamanca, 1981. Carmen Codoñer Merino & Juan Antonio González Iglesias (eds.), *Antonio de Nebrija: Edad Media y Renacimiento*, Salamanca, Ediciones Universidad de Salamanca, 1994.

²⁶³ We can mention other inquisitive humanists, such as Lucio Marineo Sículo (1444-1536). This Sicilian scholar taught Poetry and Rhetoric for 12 years (from 1484) in the University of Salamanca. Prior to that, he had been a teacher of Greek language and literature in Palermo. His methodology consisted of some simple grammatical notions of Latin based on the direct study of the texts. *Cf.* Alicia Gould y Quincy, «Lucio Marineo Sículo (1444? 1536)», *Simancas. Estudios de Historia Moderna*, 1 (Valladolid, 1950), pp. 257-270.

²⁶⁴ «The humanist Nebrija followed the lines set by Valla and Poliziano and proposed the critical philological method as an alternative to the speculative grammar of the scholastics. His method seeks to restore the union between Grammar, Rhetoric and Dialectics in order to create a true science of discourse that maintains the original relation between words (*verbum*) and objects (*res*), and that does not wrap that relation under a forest of distinctions and words»: Cirilo Flórez Miguel, «Las ciencias y la Universidad de Salamanca en el siglo xv», p. 197.

²⁶⁵ «This is the kind of elegance sought by Valla and Nebrija, with which history becomes one of the main elements of Grammar. One of the tasks of the grammarian is to look for examples in the history of the language that act as linguistic evidence and become a fundamental element of philological grammar»: Cirilo Flórez Miguel, «Las ciencias y la Universidad de Salamanca en el siglo xv», p. 198. Inmaculada Delgado Jara & Rosa M.ª Herrera García, «Humanidades y humanistas en la Universidad de Salamanca del siglo xv», p. 263.

²⁶⁶ Esperabé, II, p. 328. The documents are unclear. They reveal that he occupied the Chair until 1523.

²⁶⁷ Esperabé, II, p. 378.

²⁶⁸ «In the century that stretches from 1406 to 1516 (or to 1529), this University, as other European counterparts, goes from being a medieval University to a modern University. The renewal of knowledge makes it possible to establish three different schools of thought. One was the scholastic line, epitomized by the «Thomist humanism» of the professors of Arts and the application of Thomas Aquinas' method to theological studies. The second was the line of philological humanism, in which thanks to Nebrija and other professors such as Arias Barbosa, Hernando Alonso and Hernán Núñez de Guzmán, modern Humanism prevails. And finally the line of innovators in the Arts studies, with the arrival of Nominalism thanks to Silíceo, and the establishment of a renovation of sciences in the famous Statutes of 1529, when Pérez de Oliva was the Rector»: Cirilo Flórez Miguel, «Presentación», in *La primera Escuela de Salamanca (1406-1516)*, Salamanca, Universidad de Salamanca, 2012, p. 11. For a literary overview of that time, see Fernando Gómez Redondo, *Historia de la prosa de los Reyes Católicos, umbral del Renacimiento*, Madrid, Cátedra, 2012, 2 vols.

²⁶⁹ Francisco Vindel, *El arte tipográfico en España durante el siglo xv: Salamanca, Coria y Reino de Galicia*, Madrid, Dirección General de Relaciones Culturales, 1946.

²⁷⁰ The Senate meeting on June 1468 gives the following orders to a delegation headed for Medina del Campo: «Buy any books needed for the Library of the Studium be it texts or lessons, and charge them to the University»: *Libros de Claustros*, 1, fol. 126r; *Extractos*, p. 110.

²⁷¹ However, there must have been a previous collection, because the University Library is already mentioned in the cession document of the library of Juan Alfonso de Segovia in 1457: BUSA, ms. 211.

²⁷² Florencio Marcos Rodríguez, *Extractos*, p. 81, Senate meeting on January 3ʳᵈ 1466.

[273] Participants in the Senate meeting on December 17th 1465 discussed the 2,000 florins destined to the purchase of books, and it was decided that they should remain in the Library with their chains: *Extractos*, p. 80. On October 23rd, the Senate meeting establishes that the Library had to open two hours after the Prime lessons and one hour and a half after three o'clock in the afternoon (Vespers): *Extractos*, p. 103. In a visit to the Library on May 28th 1471, an inventory of 201 volumes was made: *Extractos*, p. 150. *Cf. Libros de Claustros*, 1, fols. 115v, 193. In August 1472, Master Pascual Ruiz and the bachelor Quintanilla, who were in charge of the Library, put in it «on a bench, to the left of the chest, a compilation of texts on Moral Philosophy and a compilation on the whole text of the *De Generatione*» together with other books of Medicine by some Arab authors and some questions by Buridan on the *Physics. Cf. Libros de Claustros*, 1, fol. 229.

[274] The members of the academic Senate of Salamanca agreed, on September 15th 1469, to lend the Bishop of Salamanca, Gonzalo de Vivero, a book of Medicine «by Arnaldus, so that he can have it written»; that is, to have it copied: *Libros de Claustros*, 1, fol. 166v; *Extractos*, p. 132.

[275] The donation of books by the Canon Alonso Ortiz, from Toledo, to the University in 1508, was so substantial (almost one thousand books) for its time «that it led the Senate to erect a new building to keep them»: *Bulario*, I, p.176, 187.

[276] *Bulario*, I, p. 174. The first complete inventory of the Library of the Cathedral chapter dates from 1533: Florencio Marcos Rodríguez, «La antigua biblioteca de la catedral de Salamanca», *op. cit.* Also, there are references to a system of book loans and renting among the members of the Cathedral chapter: Susana Guijarro González, «La formación cultural del clero catedralicio en la Salamanca medieval (siglos XII al XV)», *op.cit.*, p. 460.

[277] Ramón Hernández Martín, «El convento y Estudio de San Esteban», p. 598.

[278] Archives of the University of Salamanca (AUSA), *Libros de Claustros*, 1, fol. 222.

[279] The Senate meeting on June 13th 1472 registered an agreement to begin the construction of the Library «Because it has been a long time since the Library was planned but the works did not start». Marcos Rodríguez, *Extractos*, pp. 166, 291. *Libros de Claustros*, 3, fol. 86.

[280] Lucía Lahoz is the researcher who has most vehemently defended the permanent location of the University Chapel where it now is, at least since 1429, against the traditional opinions that proposed the existence of a first oratory in the hallway of the East entrance of the Escuelas Mayores building. With regard to the paintings on the vault of the Library, the first known description comes from the Sicilian humanist Lucio Marineo Sículo, who taught in Salamanca from 1484 to 1496, and his book *De Hispaniae laudibus*, Burgos, 1497: «Here is the Library, which is beautiful. Spectators are delighted with its vault, which shows a starry night, the planets and a canopy of heaven with all the constellations in the zodiac. This vault is closed and surrounded by a stone construction. Light enters the library through glass windows. In front of the door there was a long and beautiful ambulatory, which was intended for strolling». *Cf.* Lucía Lahoz, «La imagen de la Universidad de Salamanca en el Cuatrocientos», in *Salamanca y su Universidad en el primer Renacimiento: siglo XV. Miscelánea Alfonso IX*, 2010, Salamanca, Ediciones Universidad de Salamanca, 2011, pp. 298-299. It seems that this vault or «Sky of Salamanca» shows the arrangement of the stars when the Library was created, in August 1475. However, other authors propose that the date matches a stay of the Catholic Monarchs in the town. *Cf.* José María Martínez Frías, *El cielo de Salamanca. La bóveda de la antigua Biblioteca universitaria*, Salamanca, Ediciones Universidad de Salamanca, 2006.

[281] The plan has been attributed to Ruiz de Aranda, professor of Natural Philosophy; García Villadiego, professor of Canon Law; the Jewish astronomer Abraham Zacut; Antonio de Nebrija, professor of Grammar; Pedro Martínez de Osma, professor of Philosophy and Theology; Diego Torres, professor of Astronomy… We have to take into account the fact that in Salamanca in the second half of the 15th century there was a consolidated scientific school; Cirilo Flórez Miguel, Pablo García Castillo & Roberto Albares, *El Humanismo científico*, Salamanca, Caja de Ahorros Provincial, 1988. Extended re-edition, 1999.

[282] «In the University there is a sacred place which has outstanding gilt coffering and which is used for worship and for the holy sacrifice of the mass. There, they keep the funds of the University as if it were a treasury, and they hold board meetings»: Statement by Luicio Marineo towards 1496, quoted by Felipe Pereda, *La arquitectura elocuente. El edificio de la Universidad de Salamanca bajo el reinado de Carlos V*, Madrid, Sociedad Estatal para la Conmemoración de los Centenarios de Felipe II y Carlos V, 2000, pp. 19-20.

[283] Mariano Peset & Pilar García Trobat, «Poderes y modelos universitarios, siglos XV-XIX», p. 55.

[284] Royal Decree, Medina del Campo, June 18th 1504: Esperabé, I, p. 356.

[285] The memory of corporative exemptions was still alive in 1512, when the University defined itself as an exempt ecclesiastical corporation during the visit of Diego Ramírez de Villaescusa. *Cf.* M.ª Paz Alonso Romero, «El fuero universitario, siglos XIII-XIX», *op. cit.*, p. 175.

[286] Manuel Fernández Álvarez, «La reforma universitaria [de 1512]», *Stvdia Historica. Historia Moderna*, II, 3 (Salamanca, 1984), pp. 21-46.

[287] Pope Leo X interpreted the first constitution of Martin V and established that the position of Rector and counsiliaries of the University of Salamanca could not be occupied by people who came from Salamanca or who had lived there for ten years without belonging to the Studium, or from relatives of noblemen and rich people; Rome, December 3rd 1518: *Bulario*, I, p. 191 & *Bulario*, III, pp. 228-229.

[288] Adrian VI authorized students of Canons and Laws in Salamanca to become bachelors in the University after five years of study; Rome, September 12th 1522: *Bulario*, III, pp. 231-232. In his *Bulario*, I, p. 191, Beltrán de Heredia offers a wrong interpretation of this bull: «He reduced to five years the six years of studies and practice that, according to the Constitution, must take place for bachelors to become graduates in Canons and Laws».

[289] The (unconfirmed) statutes of 1529 show a certain precaution against the interference of the Cathedral chapter in the Rector appointment: «The Rector has to be elected according to what is established in the corresponding Constitution, and he cannot be a person from the Cathedral chapter of Salamanca»: *Estatutos de la Universidad de Salamanca, 1529, mandato de Pérez de Oliva, rector*, edited by José Luis Fuertes Herreros, Salamanca, Ediciones Universidad de Salamanca, 1984.

[290] Mariano Peset & Pilar García Trobat, «Poderes y modelos universitarios, siglos XV-XIX», p. 57. The Statutes of 1538 banned members of the Colleges from occupying the position of Rector of the University.

[291] We can point out the discrepancies between the research of José Luis Fuentes, who has highlighted the statutory validity of the visit of 1529; and the research of Pilar Valero, who interprets the visit as an unfinished reform with no official ratification. *Cf.* José Luis Fuertes Herreros, *Estatutos de la Universidad de Salamanca, 1529*, Salamanca, Ediciones Universidad de Salamanca, 1984; Pilar Valero García, «Un aspecto del rectorado de Fernán

Pérez de Oliva, pretendidos estatutos de la Universidad de Salamanca bajo su mandato», *Stvdia Historica. Historia Moderna*, IV, 3 (Salamanca, 1986), pp. 51-74.

[292] Paul III authorized the University Senate of Salamanca to reform the Constitutions with the agreement of two thirds of the votes; Rome, October 26th 1543: *Bulario*, III, p. 288.

[293] Paul III confirmed the agreement established between the University of Salamanca and the College of San Bartolomé with regard to the masters and doctors that were to be members of the examining board of the graduate exams for members of the College; Rome, July 16th 1540: *Bulario*, III, pp. 281-282. Paul III confirmed the statute of the University Senate of Salamanca that described who had to be present in the graduate exams; and he safeguarded the rights of those who had appealed to the Apostolic See; Rome, August 5th 1541: *Bulario*, III, pp. 283-285. Pontifical confirmation of the statute agreed in the Senate of the University of Salamanca regarding the distribution of subjects that would be taught each year by the professors of Canons and Laws; Rome, May 26th 1549: *Bulario*, III, pp. 292-294.

[294] The Statutes of 1538 became a complement to the medieval Constitutions of 1422, which now had been renovated, qualified and updated in several points. They were printed with the following title: *Statutes created by the University of Salamanca [Estatutos hechos por la Universidad de Salamanca]*, Salamanca, MDXXXVIII, 32 pages. There are no references to its passing by the Council of Castile, which would explain their later revision in the Statutes of Covarrubias of 1561, when the Monarchs had finally asserted their authority over the aspirations of autonomy of the corporation. A modern transcription in Spanish of the Statutes of 1538 can be found in Enrique Esperabé de Arteaga, *Historia pragmática e interna de la Universidad de Salamanca*, I, Salamanca, 1914, pp. 139-215.

[295] The details of the creation of this plenary board are unclear due to the loss of some minute books of the meetings from this period: 1482-1502, 1513-1525 and 1536-1538.

[296] The first ledger or book of *Cuentas Generales* that is kept in the University Archive comprises the period 1518-1526 (AUSA. 1243). The annual income from the Tercias is as follows: 1518-1519, 2,568,620 maravedís; 1519-1520, 2,467,916; 1520-1521, 2,497,080; 1521-1522, 2,836,896 maravedís. The annual average is 2,592,628 maravedís. Based on the data from Fernando Martín Lamouroux, *La revelación contable en la Salamanca historica, op. cit.*, pp. 199-200.

[297] Bull «copiosus in misericordia» of Rome, June 15th 1504, in which the Order of San Benito of Valladolid joins the Priory of San Vicente of Salamanca (and separates from Cluny). Observance is established and it becomes a University hall of residence for twenty members of the Order: *Bulario*, I, p. 189 and Bulario, III, pp. 212-213.

[298] Founding bull for the College of Cuenca in Salamanca, with an authorization to grant degrees in all the faculties and the granting of the same privileges as the College of San Bartolomé in Salamanca and the Colleges of Santa Cruz and San Gregorio in Valladolid; Rome, April 25th 1523: *Bulario*, III, pp. 234-236.

[299] Pontifical authorization for the Archbishop of Toledo, Alfonso de Fonseca, to fund a college in Salamanca with the privileges of all the other existing Colleges; Rome, October 13th 1525: *Bulario*, III, pp. 243-245. Granting for Alfonso de Fonseca, Archbishop of Toledo, to annex the benefices from the dioceses of Toledo and Salamanca to his College of Santiago in Salamanca; Rome, May 3rd 1532: *Bulario*, III, pp. 260-261.

[300] On January 28th 1506, members of the Senate «ordered to demolish the floor of the Library so that the entire hall becomes a Chapel, from

ceiling to floor, and that the Library is erected somewhere else»: *Libros de Claustros*, 4, fol. 173. Perhaps, the donation of the library of the Canon Alonso Ortiz, from Toledo, to the University, with nearly 1,000 volumes, contributed to this decision. The books arrived in March 1508: Beltrán de Heredia, «La Universidad en el siglo xv», *Cartulario*, II, pp. 212-213, 215. In any case, a new altarpiece for the Chapel had been already contracted with Felipe Bigarny in September 15th 1503. The altarpiece would include sculptures of Saint Jerome, the Fathers of the Latin Church, Saint Thomas Aquinas or the Immaculate Conception/Assumption of Mary. The paintings of the altarpiece were assigned to Juan de Flandes, who finished them in 1507. José M.ª Martínez Frías, «La Real Capilla de San Jerónimo», in *Loci et imagines, imágenes y lugares. 800 años de patrimonio de la Universidad de Salamanca*, Salamanca, Ediciones Universidad de Salamanca, pp. 67-107.

[301] The façade was built in the decade of 1520, and we know that it was finished in 1528. In her research on the figure of Juan de Álava, Ana Castro registers a heavy spending of the University in the ledgers of 1523 and 1524: Ana Castro Santamaría; *Juan de Álava, arquitecto del Renacimiento*, Salamanca, Caja Duero, 2001. This new era gave way to other building feats, such as the new Escuelas Menores, which were finished in 1533. In February 1510, the old building had «lost its auditoriums», but as the works of the Library had already started, the University decided that «a new building will not be created until the Library is finished»: Plenary meeting on Februrary 7th 1510; *cf.* Beltrán de Heredia, «La Universidad en el siglo xv», *Cartulario*, II, p. 200.

[302] Some authors have defended the stimulating hypothesis that the façade was designed and funded by the Chancellery of Charles V after the Revolt of the Comuneros, in which the University had played an important role. The façade would therefore represent a glorification of the Emperor, as in the Alcázar of Toledo, another town that housed comuneros. Oddly enough, there are no references to this façade in the minute books of the Senate meetings in the University Archive since from year 1525, the date from when they have first survived: Paulette Gabaudan, *El mito imperial. Estudio iconológico de los relieves de la Universidad salmantina*, Madrid, Éride Ediciones, 2012, pp. 31, 146-147. After the return of the Emperor to Spain in 1523, some counselors had urged him to punish the rebellious towns: «To take the market away from Medina del Campo, the Chancellery from Valladolid or the University from Salamanca», in Manuel Fernández Álvarez, *Carlos V. El César y el hombre*, Madrid, Espasa Calpe, 1999, p. 285. In 1536, Leopoldo de Austria, uncle of the Emperor Charles, became Rector of the University: Esperabé, II, p. 8.

[303] Salustiano de Dios, «Los juristas de Salamanca en el siglo xv», p. 61: «...the development of the most Catholic and Noble Empire, which is based on the lack of equality of people before the Law. The University of Salamanca was linked to the Empire, for better or for worse, and at its service, as is proclaimed in the coats of arms of its most emblematic buildings, which can still be seen today».

FINAL NOTE: This work has been created in the framework of the National Project of the Spanish Ministry of Economy and Competitiveness, «Las Universidades Hispánicas (siglos xv-xix. España, Portugal, Italia y México. Historia, saberes e imagen»: HAR2012-30663.

In the Salmantinian workshops of Gráficas Lope, beyond the Tormes River,
the printing of this book was finished on the 18th day of October of the
year 2013, on the festivity of Saint Luke, much celebrated by
courtesans and students, and not *Bologna* nor any other
power in this world have cast a shadow over the old
university saying that stated and (still) states that
«From St. Luke's day to Yuletide, few real
students can be seen outside».
So be it.